"Twau twau or Meearmee traditions.
(denominated in Gov. Dinwiddie's speech, nov. 1752, Twightwees,
and in a treaty at Lancaster in 1748 – ʃ

The original name of the tribe was Twaatwaa, sometimes pronounced
Twau twau. The origin of this name is thus accounted for.
In an early period of their existence they discovered the Cherokees, and were
in the habit of making war upon them. They had attacked them three
different times, when the Cherokees resolved to retaliate. They came to
a large river where they discovered upon the bank a single track. They
crossed and upon the opposite shore they saw other tracks. Continuing the march they found at a distance other tracks, and so on
at intervals, until at length they saw, blazed upon the side of a
tree the head and neck of a Crane. They came to a prairie
where they saw two of these animals and driving them before them
party they crossed. The Miamies were ambuscaded on the
opposite side and when the Cherokees approached the

OCCASIONAL CONTRIBUTIONS FROM THE MUSEUM OF
ANTHROPOLOGY OF THE UNIVERSITY OF MICHIGAN
No. 7

MEEĀRMEEAR TRADITIONS

BY

C. C. TROWBRIDGE

EDITED BY VERNON KINIETZ

ANN ARBOR
UNIVERSITY OF MICHIGAN PRESS
April, 1938

© 1938 by the Regents of the University of Michigan
The Museum of Anthropology
All rights reserved

ISBN (print): 978-1-949098-57-0
ISBN (ebook): 978-1-951538-56-9

Browse all of our books at
sites.lsa.umich.edu/archaeology-books.

Order our books from the University of Michigan
Press at www.press.umich.edu.

For permissions, questions, or manuscript queries,
contact Museum publications by email at umma-
pubs@umich.edu or visit the Museum website at
lsa.umich.edu/ummaa.

FOREWORD

A manuscript entitled "Meeārmeear Traditions" and a letter by its author, C. C. Trowbridge, transmitting it to his chief, Governor Lewis Cass, in the possession of the Burton Historical Collection of the Detroit Public Library, offered so much information on a now extinct tribe that it was decided to publish this material. There were one hundred and forty pages, six and one-fourth inches by seven and one-fourth in the manuscript; and six pages, seven and one-half inches by nine and one-half in the letter.

This report on the traditions of the Miamis as well as a similar study of the Wyandots was written in 1824–25 by Trowbridge at the instigation of Cass to aid in settling a dispute between these tribes as to precedence of settlement in the region they then occupied in Ohio and Indiana.

The beginnings of this work are found in a pamphlet published by Cass about 1820 and reprinted in 1823. This questionnaire is not now known in its original form, but the second edition bore the title *Inquiries respecting the History, Traditions, Languages, Manners, Customs, Religion, &c. of the Indians, living within the United States.**

These questionnaires were distributed throughout his jurisdiction to all traders and Indian agents. The number of replies received and their disposition is unknown. Most of the copies of the questionnaire have also disappeared. Schoolcraft† wrote a review of the *Inquiries* in which he mentioned that he understood that several valuable replies had been received. A reply to the linguistic portion of the questionnaire, written by Schoolcraft on the Chippewa, was listed by James C. Pilling‡ as being in the possession of J. G. Shea.

* Detroit: Sheldon and Reed, 1823, 64 pp.
† *North American Review*, 45 (1837): 58–59.
‡ "Bibliography of the Algonquian Languages," *Bur. Amer. Ethnol. Bull.*, 13 (1891): 454.

Trowbridge followed the questionnaire in the arrangement of subject matter in his report on the traditions of the Miamis. A comparison of "An Account of the Manners and Customs of the Sauk and Fox Nations of Indian Traditions," by Thomas Forsyth,* with this report shows that Forsyth also followed the Cass pamphlet.

The distribution of questionnaires may not have originated with Cass, but it is interesting to note that the same technique was subsequently used by Schoolcraft, Morgan, and Powell.

"Meearmeear Traditions" is given here as it appears in manuscript. Trowbridge was rushed in transcribing his notes as he explained in his covering letter to Cass, which doubtless accounts for most of the inconsistencies of spelling, the misspellings, and the omissions of words. Some omissions and necessary corrections have been supplied within brackets. Material within parentheses and footnotes marked with an asterisk were so designated by Trowbridge.

The phonetic symbols marking the Miami words are given as they appear. At the end of the paper there is a table of phonetic values worked out with the counsel of C. F. Voegelin.

Trowbridge mentioned only two informants by name, Le Gros and Richardville, so it would appear that if there were others at least these were the most important.

Grateful acknowledgments are made to the Burton Historical Collection for permission to publish this very interesting report and letter, and to the Horace H. Rackham School of Graduate Studies for the grant which made the publication possible.

* Emma H. Blair, ed., *Indian Tribes of the Upper Mississippi* (Cleveland: Arthur H. Clark Co., 1912), 2: 183–245.

CONTENTS

Biographical Sketch	ix
The Covering Letter to General Cass	1
Meeārmeear Traditions	6
Twau Twau or Meearmée Traditions	6
Government	13
War and Its Incidents	19
Peace	27
Death and Its Incidents	30
Birth and Its Incidents	37
Marriage and Its Incidents	41
Family Government &c.	46
Medecine	48
Astronomy &c.	50
Religion	51
General Manners &c.	57
Games, Dances & Amusements	59
Food, Mode of Living &c.	64
Hunting	66
Feasts & Fasts	66
Miscellaneous	68
A Tale — Founded on Fact	70
The Young Thunder Spirits	72
A Weeau Tale	73
Le Gros's Account of the Medecine Society	77
Man Eaters	88
Table of Phonetic Values	91

BIOGRAPHICAL SKETCH

Charles Christopher Trowbridge was born in Albany, New York, December 29, 1800. He moved westward to Detroit in 1819. The next spring he joined General Cass in his expedition among the Upper Great Lakes and Mississippi tribes in the capacity of clerk and assistant topographer. Henry Rowe Schoolcraft,* also a member of the party, published a narrative journal of the expedition. Shortly after the return of the group Trowbridge became the private secretary of General Cass. As such he accompanied Eleazar Williams to Green Bay in 1821 to arrange for the purchase of lands for the Oneida and Stockbridge tribes. On his return from Green Bay he was given the post of assistant secretary of the local Indian department. Since his first arrival in Detroit he had been the deputy of Major Rowland, who was the United States marshal, clerk of the courts, justice of the peace, and trustee of the city. Trowbridge was also made secretary of the Board of Regents of the University of Michigan.

Through his position in the Indian department and as the Governor's secretary, he had many contacts with the Indian tribes throughout the Territory of Michigan, in treaty negotiations, payment of annuities, location of schools and blacksmiths in accord with treaties, and other matters, including making confidential reports to Cass on the administration of the heads of agencies.

In 1823 he was sent to Green Bay to take temporary charge of the Indian agency during the sickness of the agent, Commodore Brevoort. While there he compiled an ethnology of the Menominees and a vocabulary with grammatical notes of their language. This is still in manuscript.

* *Narrative Journal of Travels Through the Northwestern Regions of the United States* (Albany: E. and E. Hosford, 1821), pp. 1-419.

The winter of 1823-24 found him engaged in a study of the traditions and customs of the Delawares. The following winter was spent in a similar study of the Miamis. In 1825 he dropped all of his former occupations except that of accountant in the Indian department, and devoted himself to business pursuits such as banking, land development, and sawmills.

He was mayor of Detroit in 1834. In 1837 he was nominated by the Whigs as governor of the State and defeated by a majority of two hundred and thirty-seven by Stevens T. Mason, who appointed him a regent of the University of Michigan in 1839, which office he held until 1842.

In all of the documents that I have examined he signed his name "C. C. Trowbridge." In the *Michigan Pioneer Collections* he is referred to as Charles Christopher and also Charles Chester, but the former appears to be correct. He died April 3, 1883.*

* For a more complete account of his life on which this sketch is based, see James V. Campbell, "Biographical Sketch of Charles Christopher Trowbridge," *Mich. Pioneer Coll.*, 6 (1907 reprint): 478-91.

THE COVERING LETTER
TO GENERAL CASS

FORT WAYNE, 6 March 1825

MY DEAR GOVERNOR.

A sense of your anxiety to see and examine the report of my labours among the Miamies, induced me to use unremitting industry in transcribing from my notes, so that I might sieze the first opportunity to transmit it to you. Upon the arrival of a stranger from St. Louis on his way to Detroit I redoubled my exertions, and a day or two since committed them to his hands. You can better imagine that I can describe my surprize and mortification, when, upon the morning following his departure the traveller returned, the Indians having stolen every thing he possessed, while he was absent from his encampment in search of his horse. M. Kercheval & myself accompanied him to the spot (about twenty miles distant) and at an Indian hut a few miles further, we had the good fortune to find every thing safe. I possessed myself again of my papers, (having changed my opinion of their bearer) and hold them for another and a safer opportunity, if one should offer. In the mean time I do myself the honour to acknowledge the receipt of your letters of the 6th and 13. Feby, as well as of that by Richard, which came to hand a few days ago.

The present necessary to make Le Gros[1] was so small (being but thirty dollars) that I thought you would dislike to be troubled with paying it, and therefore requested

---

[1] One of the villages of the Miamis on the Wabash was called "Les gros" according to Sabrevois in 1718, "Memoir on the Savages of Canada as far as the Mississippi River, and Describing their Customs and Manners," *Wis. Hist. Coll.*, 16 (1902): 376. This village was undoubtedly named for its chief whose name was the same as that of Trowbridge's informant and who may possibly have been one of his ancestors. Le Gros died December 22, 1826.

Genl. Tipton[2] to do so. I believe the old man is perfectly satisfied. I have endeavoured to economise as much as possible, and the whole of the expenses thus far, to be allowed to the agency, do not exceed ninety dollars.

A recent visit from Le Gros has enabled me to obtain some further information from him on the several subjects mentioned in the letters from you with which I have been last honored; and I have annexed to my observations upon the Miami language a tabular list of the names, in that dialect, of the surrounding nations, and also a statement exhibiting the affinities of other languages to the Miami. With respect to the latter, I take the liberty to suggest for your consideration, the opinion that according to your scale, the degrees of affinity are graduated, not more by the absolute and original similarity of dialect, than by the opportunities of the respective tribes for conference and association. I mean that this is the case between those tribes which are not connected by the ties of blood. For instance, the Miamies understand perfectly the Kaskaskias, Peorias, Weas & Piankeshaws, because those tribes have all descended from them. And the difference of dialect is scarcely more than between the present Parisian and the Canadian french. They understand the Kickapoos tolerably well, because, although originally of the Shawnee stock (and possessing in common with them and the Sacs, the *th* as in Teek$\overline{um}$the) they have become incorporated with the Miamies by intermarriages and have greatly assimilated to them in manners and language. They did not understand the Delawares, Shawnees Ottawas, Potawatamies, Chippeways, Sacs & Osages, until their occupation of hunting, trading, making war and treaties brought them into contact with each other and they acquired by practice, the art of speaking the different languages which possessed many similarities enabling them to catch the words and sounds with facility. And finally, they do not at all comprehend the Iroquois, Wyandot, Wineeb$\overline{aa}$goa,

[2] Indian agent at Fort Wayne, Indiana.

Sioux Minōaminee, Creeks, Choctaws or Cherokees — either because their languages are "radically different", or because they have had little connection with them.

I am aware that this militates against the grand, the sublime proposition, that all the Indian languages are derived from the same common stock; yet I have deemed it my duty to submit the observations as the substance of the Miami account. When your letters arrived I had closed that part of my report which described the successive migrations of the Miamies, and as nothing is therein said of their having once resided upon Fox river or at Detroit, I will here mention, that upon subsequent enquiry Le Gros told me that a vague and indefinite tradition existed of their once having lived in the north, but supposing it to be an unfounded tale he had forborne to mention it to me. It is possible that much has been lost from the great lapse of time, and it is cause of regret that many of their accounts on this subject want that perspicuity and minuteness of detail which would render them valuable.

They do not know that any of the Miamies have ever lived at Detroit,[3] and they disclaim the name Wauweeautonao, given to that place, alledging its origin to have been among the Potawatamies. Kaukaumeeōangee, or Keekaukaumeeōangee, is the Miami name, and means "At the strait". It is compounded of Keekaukaumēekee ("the river between two lakes", from Kitshēekaumee a Lake) and the prepositional termination ōangee, "at the". —

I have repeatedly questioned Le Gros about "trees of peace", and particularly since the receipt of your last letters. He says he never heard before that the Indians, in any instance, marked the boundaries of their hunting lands. "Yet, continues he, Awaandeeōanee Tauwaūnee (a peace tree) was once planted upon the St. Joseph's, by the Chippeways, Ottawas, Potawatamies and Miamies. It was a white poplar.

[3] Several households and families of Miamis settled at Detroit in 1703 and incorporated themselves with the Hurons, according to Cadillac in his "Report of Detroit in 1703," *Mich. Pioneer Coll.*, 33 (1904): 162-63.

Under its branches a grand council was held, at which a general method of government was agreed upon for the respective nations, and to that effect certain fundamental laws were passed, which have been since immutable. There, a general alliance, offensive and defensive, was made; and although the tree be now physically dead, it yet lives green in the hearts of the Indians". I regret that Le Gros is unable to furnish me with the particulars of this very interesting tradition.[4]

The idea which you have been pleased to suggest with respect to the division of the Miamies into Miamies & Eel rivers, by the late Capt. Wells, corresponds with an account which I have heard; but the Wüyautōnoakee or Weas, were not made a separate tribe for the same purposes: *Their* separation was long, long before, and was the effect of chance.

It is a matter of but little surprise to me that Charlevoix should have called the Mascoutins *gens de feu*, since there is so much likeness in sound between M'skōataa a prairie and Skōataa, fire. I have been unable to obtain any more information on the subject of these people than I have already submitted, yet I hope the Kickapoo, if he comes, will set the matter at rest. My first messenger to this man brought word that he was afraid to come, and I have since sent again, the speech of the agent being accompanied by one from Richardville,[5] so that I have strong hopes of seeing him with the messenger, whose return is looked for hourly. Nothing but this now prevents me from repairing to Wapaghkonetta,[6] on my way to Detroit.

[4] Such an alliance was very old among the Chippewas, Ottawas, and Potawatomies. An alliance between these tribes and the Wyandots was entered into about 1720 according to Peter D. Clarke, *Origin and Traditional History of the Wyandots* (Toronto: Hunter, Rose and Co., 1870), p. 17. I am unable to determine the date of the alliance here reported.

[5] Pee-ge-wa or Richard Ville signed the Treaty of Greenville, August 3, 1795, for the Miamis. See "Treaty of Peace between the United States and the Indians," *Mich. Pioneer Coll.*, 20 (1912, reprint): 418.

[6] Wapakoneta was a Shawnee village established by the consent of the Miamis on the site of the present Wapakoneta, Auglaize County, Ohio.

My mind has long laboured with and soon would have brought forth the idea mentioned in your letter of the 13th. ultimo, viz: that there exists more difference in the manner of utterance than in the different dialects of the Indians *around us*, Hence we may find more affinities when they are spread upon paper leisurely, than when heard with all the different modulations of voice common to the different tribes. Another difference which is supposed to be considerable, is to be found in the verbal terminations and affixes. In the Chippeway the past tense is known by the addition of *bun*. In the Delaware the past ends in *aap, aup* or *oap* and the future in *tsh*, while the Miami is distinguished by *pau* and *kart*, or *kārt*. In case the Kickapoo should not come soon, I shall go to the Shawnee village and return here, with a view to meet any instructions which you may be pleased to transmit on the subject. I should not hezitate, if you thought best, to descend the Wabash with an Interpreter, yet at the same [time] I would regret the necessity of such a step, if it prevented me from going eastward again this spring.

I beg you to pardon the freedom with which I write, and believe me

    My dear Governor
      to be your affectionate servant
          C. C. TROWBRIDGE

His Excellency
 LEWIS CASS

MEEĀRMEEAR TRADITIONS

TWAU TWAŪ OR MEEARMÉE TRADITIONS

(Denominated in Gov. Dinwiddies speech, Nov. 1752 and in a treaty at Lancaster in 1748 — Twightwees.)

THE original name of the tribes was *Twaatwāā* sometimes pronounced Twau twaū. The origin of this name is thus accounted for. In an early period of their existence they discovered the Cherokees, and were in the habit of making war upon them. They had attacked them three different times, when the Cherokees resolved to retaliate. They came to a large river where they discovered upon the bank a single track. They crossed and upon the opposite shore they saw other tracks. Continuing the march they found at a distance other tracks, and so on at intervals, until at length they saw, blazed upon the side of a tree, the head and neck of a Crane. They came to a prairie where they saw two of these animals and driving them before the party they crossed. The Miamies were ambuscaded on the opposite side and when the Cherokees approached the Cranes began to make a noise, crying out as they do when frightened. At length the Miamies rushed upon the Cherokees and the Cranes being in the middle became much terrified and increasing their noise cried out more rapidly *Twau Twaū, Twaū Twaū* and flew off. Every Cherokee but one was killed and when he escaped to his village he told his friends that they need not wonder at their frequent defeats, for they were conquered, not by men, but by the *Twau twau's* who could fly off at will — They retained this name for a long time, when from some cause or circumstance not known they exchanged it for that of Pigeon, *Meemeeā*, which has grown by use into *Meeärmēe*.[1]

[1] The first mention of the Miami in the early accounts is by Gabriel Druillettes, *Relation ....for 1657-58*, *Jesuit Relations and Allied Documents*,

MEEARMEEAR TRADITIONS 7

But still the national mark is the head and neck of the *Tshe tsha kwau* or Crane, from which the name given them was originally derived.

They sprung up at St. Joseph's but whether they have any distinct idea of their creation, or dislike to disclose it, I cannot determine, as they profess ignorance on the subject. How long they remained there is unknown but their first removal was to Fort Wayne, where they were found by the french. The earliest incident in their history which they recollect is the arrival of the french in the lakes. The Wyandots who then lived upon Lake Huron, sent word to the Miamies and Potawatamies, that a strange people had arrived there, whom they feared because they were white and had long beards, and that they desired the assistance of their bretheren to destroy them. When the Miamies & Potawatamies arrived they found four vessels loaded with french. The three nations ambuscaded and when the visitors had disembarked they attacked and destroyed them. A few remained in one of the vessels who hoisted sail and made their escape. Then the Wyandots told their allies. "You see brothers that these people tho' they look like them, cannot be manitoos. They are unlike us, and their design in coming here must certainly be evil. We have placed the tomahawk in your hands, and you are now prepared to defend yourself against them. In the mean time if any more should arrive, we shall probably want your assistance in repelling them."[2] They next saw the whites at Detroit when they held a council with them and made peace.[3]

---

ed. Reuben Goldthwaites (Cleveland, Ohio: The Burrows Brothers, 1899), 44: 247, who called them the "Oumamik" and the "Outitchakouk," the latter being the Atchatchakangouen or "crane people."

[2] There is no counterpart of this story in the French documents.

[3] The first Frenchman to report meeting the Miamis was Radisson, who found them westward of Green Bay about 1658. Perrot found them in the same region six or seven years later. The first record of the French meeting the Miamis on the strait between Lakes Huron and Erie was in 1687 when De la Durantaye read a proclamation repeating the claim of France to possession of that country.

They have been at war with the Pawnees, Cherokees, Chickasaws, Choctaws, Iroquois (whom they call Senecas) and Osages. They have never been at war with the Potawatamies, Ottawas, Chippewas, Wyandots or Delawares. To this there are two exceptions. One after the english took possession of Detroit, when a trader who resided at Cincinnati became jealous of another who lived at Piqua and instigated the Miamies to rob him of his merchandise. The english employed the Chippeways to avenge this insult and they attacked the hunting camps of the Miamies and took prisoners two women. The Miamies pursued them down the Miami river to Roche de Bon [Bout?] where they had a battle, and afterwards they made a peace by advice of the English, having rescued the prisoners.

The other exception was that of a slight difficulty which occurred between them and the Shawnees in consequence of the latter having joined the Cherokees against them. But no serious difficulty took place, and about fifty years ago a peace was made, which has not since been violated. Richardville recollects the time when difficulties were settled, in consequence of one of the war chiefs having spent a winter among the Cherokees (or Kotōawhau), Shawnees and *Moshkoas* or *Creeks*, with a view to arrange the preliminaries. A general alliance existed anciently among the northern nations including the Miamies, Wyandots, Delawares, Shawnees, Chippeways & Potawatamies, against the southern tribes, ie the Cherokees, Choctows, Creeks, Chickasaws and also the Iroquois.

Before leaving the St. Josephs a party of two or three hundred Miamies sat out to hunt, as well for game as to know if there were not other nations living in the country, whom they had not seen. They reached an immense prairie now called the grand Kickapoo prairie, on the Wabash, and passing through it they discovered as they thought a herd of Buffaloes. The chief called upon his young men to go and kill some of them, that they might furnish themselves with provisions. Upon descending a little hill one of the party who had remained behind ran forward and suggested to the pursuers that he tho! the Buffaloes which they saw were men. The chief was surprized and immediately despatched two young men by a circuitous route, to ascertain whether they were in fact Buffaloes, or men in disguise. The young men went as they were directed and upon approaching near, discovered the Indians employed in painting their bodies with red clay. The messengers returned to the chief and related what they had seen and the Miamies prepared to attack them. They made an attack but they found it impossible to kill them, on account of large shields made of Buffaloes hides, which were carried by their opponents, and covered them from head to foot, being altogether impenatrable by arrows. These Indians were the Osages. They frequently threw dust into the air, upon the approach of the Miamies, with a view to induce the belief that they were in fact Buffaloes, and engaged in play. During the battle an Osage and a Miamie advanced in front of their several parties and commenced fighting with their Pukamaugun's or War clubs. The battle was long contested, but at length the Miami succeeded in killing his adversary. As soon as this personal combat was terminated two others, an Osage and a Miami, advanced with spears in their hands and commenced another battle. The Osage having seven or eight spears in his hands could not make them enter the flesh of his advarsary who had but two and of course a great advantage in this respect. In this combat, as in the other the Miami was victorious. Then one of the Osages came forward with a view to address the Miamies, but they could not understand each other, and by mutual consent, expressed in signs the battle terminated and the combatants returned to their several homes. They never knew the Indians to use shields but on the occasion just mentioned.

Since coming to Fort Wayne near which they first built a village after leaving St. Joseph's they have had few wars with the Indians around them. The Cherokees are the only Indians against whom they maintained a war for any time.

They possessed formerly a large number of belts and pipes illustrative of different events in their history. Two boxes containing these were burnt accidentally at the time of Harmers defeat, and with them went their early history and traditions. Before their knowledge of the whites they used belts made of the small bones found in the legs of swans and other large birds, which were attached by means of a cord composed of the fibres of the wild nettle. These were made with much labour, and were said to be admirably wrought. They soon exchanged them however for the wampum and to the loss of the chests alluded to they attribute their ignorance of their early history.

The settlement on the point, at the confluence of the St. Marys and St. Josephs was formed by a party of brothers called* *Mauma waazāukee*. The whole nation did not remove at the same time, for their villages were scattered throughout the country, among the northern nations. After they had been at Fort Wayne some time, great accessions were made to their numbers, and at one time the village contained 3000 men. Even at that time it was supposed to be but a small part of the nation. They had a village after this on the Big Miami and another upon White river.

When the first party had left St. Josephs for the Miami they encamped at the Elk's heart. An Elk was killed there and a woman who got possession of the heart hung it upon a tree; another woman stole it, and when the other came to seek her property she lamented the loss so much that the river thence took it name of Elk's Heart.

They were so numerous at St. Joseph's as to make the migration of a part of the tribe necessary. Accordingly one man separated himself from them and went to the Wabash, where he settled himself at a place now called the *Wēeau* prairie, about 20 miles below the mouth of the Tippecanoe, on the southern shore. His name was Wŭyoakeetonwau, which has since been changed to *Wŭyautonoa*, the name by which they

* It is said that this is a compound, meaning "the children of the child that cries for its mother."

MEEARMEEAR TRADITIONS

call the *Wēēaus*. (in the plural Wüyautōnoakee) — He received his name because he lived near a whirlpool in the River St. Joseph's, which in the Miami is called *Wüyōakeetonwee*.

When the *Wēēau* band had increased considerably, one of them separated himself from them and went to the mouth of the Vermillion river, where he settled down & made a village. This man had no holes or slits in his ears, as was customary at that day, and he was on that account called Piankeshaw- (Püyunkeeshāū).

Afterwards one of the Piankeshaws descended the Wabash and settled below Vincennes, at a place called by them *Tshipkohkeeōangee*, (literally "at the root") in consequence of a small shrub which grew there (Vincennes is now known by this name) — This tribe was called *Kohkōhkee*, which we pronounce Kaskāskia.

These are the tribes of Wüyāutonoa. The next one who left St. Josephs went to White River, and finding a very clear whitish spring emptying into the river upon his arrival, he gave the river its name *Waupeekomēēkee* (or *White Water*).

The third migration was made by the father of Le Gros, who went from St. Joseph's to Piqua. When they were encamped there they heard in the night a great rumbling noise, and in the morning discovered a great ravine. They followed it some distance to a lick, in the midst of the prairie, where they found a great stone, and they gave the place the name of *Usāānee* and the river, Usaanēē sēēpee. There they first met with that tribe of the Shawnees, called Pickaways. —

The fourth migration was by a hunter who descended the Miami to one of the little prairies near Fort Meigs. He made a village there and on the same ground which was occupied by General Waynes Fort or camp deposit, near Roche de Bout,[4] erected a fortification, having walls of earth and small pickets. They fortified at this place, thro' fear of the Six nations: And the place is to this day known by the Chippeways &c., by the name of Meeārmeear Wükūegon, the Miami fort.

[4] One mile above Waterville, Ohio, on the Maumee.

From the Rapids a party of about 100 went to Sandusky, where they resided a few years, but being in dread of the six nations soon returned to the fort. Another hunter travelled west to the Mississippi and being pleased with the country prevailed on his friends to accompany him. They settled near the Sacs, but soon returned to their friends. —

After this the Maumawaazaūkee came to the confluence of the Miami & St. Joseph's and settled, as has been mentioned. They were very numerous, but soon lost great numbers by sickness which they could not cure or prevent, having then no knowledge of the art of Bleeding.

Another separated from this last settlement & migrated to the west. He settled on one of the branches of the Mississippi where he found a great many swans, ducks & other water fowl, and from that circumstance the division took the name of Waupungeeōāla, or "the place of white birds."
— This branch separated & the last division was called Misoaleeaūkee or Canoe people, from the circumstance of their always hunting on the water.

There was a village on the head of Tippecanoe river. About seventy or eighty years ago the small pox destroyed all the inhabitants but an old woman and her son, an infant, who came to the Miami. The child was afterwards the chief of the turtle tribe and died not many years ago. He was called "The Grey". —

The Piankeshaws, the Weeaus (in Miami Wüautōnoakee) and the Kaskaskias (Mekoateeaukee) are descendants from the Miamies. The two first separated from them at St. Joseph's and the latter, a different tribe originally, and very poor, were discovered on the Wabash, made tributary to the discoverers and finally incorporated with them, but after sometime they separated again & divided. From these came the Peorias. These three nations speak the Miami language, but the latter by having been separated from the parent stock some time have changed their language so that there are now but few Miami words in their language. — They term these tribes their younger brothers and they claim no other actual relatives, but they have many adopted ones, viz, their elder brothers the Chippeways, their Grand fathers the Delawares, their elders brothers, the Wyandots, the Ottawuwas their elder brothers, the Potawatamies the same and the Shawnees brothers. But this arrangement seems by their account to have been a matter of trifling importance, and in accordance with the propositions of the several nations at the different councils which have been held among them.

GOVERNMENT

Their chiefs are hereditary. The course of descent is from the father to the eldest son. If a chief dies without male issue the title descends to the eldest son of his eldest daughter. In case the young chief is in minority at the death of his father or grand father, the administration of his share of the government is committed by him to his *Kaupeeau* (the Mishīnewaa of the Chippeways) if he deems him sufficiently honest and capable, or in the other event to one or more of his brother chiefs.

When the young chief has arrived at an age when he can administer the government the Kaupeeau, or the chief who has charge of the belts and other insignia of power formerly possessed by his predecessor, sends for him and offers them for his acceptance. It is common for the young man to refuse this offer, and then to assemble a party of his young friends and go out to hunt. When a considerable quantity of game has been collected he returns and makes a great feast. He sends for the *Kaupeeau* and proposes, as he is then better prepared, to accept the propostion before made to him and offers to make a handsome present for his labour and care in instructing him in the duties of a chief and the history connected with the belts, medals &c, which his father left.

The Kaupeeau then makes his arrangements for a grand council of the nation, at which he advertises them of the fact that the young man has assumed the powers and duties of his ancestor. The chief sometimes has a feast on this occasion and at others distributes large quantities of merchandize.

When in the event of the death of a chief who has no issue his Kaūpeeau is a man of information and spirit, he generally takes upon himself the discharge of the duties of the chief or is appointed thereto by the chief before his decease. The latter mode is more customary and the nation generally assents to the appointment. They have village chiefs and war chiefs, with whom the manner of descent and appointment is the same. The distinction between the village and war chiefs is considered plain. The first attends exclusively to the internal regulations of the village and to the reception of proposals for peace, while the other has the sole management of the war parties, their plans of attack &c. It is common for the war chiefs to prevent the others from joining in war parties and they tell them on these occasions to remain at home and take care of the women and children, and not to trouble themselves in matters which do not concern them in the discharge of their official duties. The situation of a chief is considered very responsible. He ought to possess a perfect equanimity of disposition and to prevent any one from discovering signs of ill humour, much less rage or anger, in his conduct. He is oftentimes obliged to submit to insults and losses of property which an ordinary member of the tribe would resent. His utensil for cooking, his horses and hunting apparatus, are at the mercy of the villagers. On the other hand, if the nation or tribe to which he belongs esteems him as a wise and a good man, they do not fail in the spring of the year to make him presents of peltry or game and thus to compensate him for some of his losses.

There are also female chiefs, both of war and of the village. They derive their powers by descent from the father who is a chief. The eldest daughter of each village and war chief is also a chief, or as the french say chefress. The duties of these female chiefs are confined to a superintendence of the preparation of nation feasts, or that part of them which is usually committed to women, to a kind of curious examination or rather watching of the affairs of the village and the conduct of the villagers, information of which they sometimes convey to the male chiefs, and to the collecting and preparing of smoked skins, moccasins, awls, sinews and other articles necessary to a war party for its convenience on the march, which they present to the leader for the benefit of the whole, before the departure of the warriors. And their power is very limited, being consequent only upon their superior powers of persuasion and the general influence which as females they have over the men of the tribe.

The *Kaūpeeau* of the Meearmēēs corresponds with the *Mishīnewaa* of the Chippeways and the *Maumeesemaukāātar* of the Shawnees. But it will be observed that he is a more distinguished character than the same officer in those nations, on account of the power given to a chief to nominate him as his successor on failure of issue. He differs from them in another respect, viz, that his office descends to his eldest son upon his demise or advance in life, unless the chief whom he serves, for good reasons should see fit to prohibit such delegation of power and appoint the successor himself. This absolute power of appointment is always reserved by the chiefs. The village chiefs as well as those of war have their respective *Kaūpeeau's*. It is their duty to carry messages for the chiefs and to divide the goods, money &c, given to the Indians at treaties. If these presents are divided among each other for the purpose of subsequent distribution among the common people, then the Kaūpeeau of each chief serves his own people; but in cases where the goods are not orginally divided by the chiefs it is common for the Kaūpeeau of one of the war chiefs to make the distribution. The Kaūpeeau of the war chief carrys the kettle and cooks the provisions of the party while on its march, and he is a kind of waiter, ready on all occasions at the call of his chief. The Kaūpeeau is wholly dependent upon the generosity and affection of his chief for compensation for his services. In dividing goods or other presents he does not reserve for himself even the common portion, but distributes the whole quantity. In the mean time however the chief generally takes from the pile a present suited to the services and merits of the Kaūpeeau.

The Kaūpeeau is not entitled to more respect on account of his office, than the young men with whom he associates in the village.

There is no particular body of counsellors in the Miami nation. On important occasions touching the sale of lands, war, or the international administration the war and village chiefs form a united council, at which the matter is debated and decided upon. It is not common for any but chiefs to visit these councils and none but chiefs ever attempt to speak in them.

There is no mode of compelling the payment of a debt. Nor do they even go so far as to sieze the property of debtors, as is practised among some others, I believe the Chippeways.

If a man commit murder, whether upon a male or female, he avoids the village of the deceased and acquaints his own father and family of the circumstance. These immediately set to work to collect a quantity of merchandize, whether of clothes, calicos, horses, wampum or whiskey, as is most convenient to the contributors. When a quantity supposed to be sufficient to pay for the deceased has been collected the father sets out to the village or wigwam of the parents of the murdered person, preceded generally by a person bearing a white flag and another with the present about to be offered. Upon his arrival he addresses the father of the deceased person, assuring him and his friends of the regret occasioned by the death, and begging them to reflect that it was the effect of liquor and probably foreordained by the great spirit and not wholly attributable to his son, who was anxious to have the matter settled. He concluded by offering the goods for the acceptance of the injured party. It is altogether optional with these to accept or refuse the offer. If the present is refused the negociation is broken off, the father and party return to their village and the murderer, who has remained at home in anxious expectation of the event, awaits the attempt of the surviving relatives of the murdered person to avenge his death. This is not omitted. Any one of the relatives who feels himself sufficiently brave or is most affected by the loss of his friend undertakes this retaliation, which is frequently repeated on the other hand and being followed up at length becomes an affair of such consequence that the intervention of the women chiefs is necessary to put a stop to the shedding of blood. This course never fails to appease those who have been last injured or suppose that they have sustained the greatest injury. It is a common saying among them that the women chiefs cannot be and seldom if ever are refused when they make a request of this description. They are more implicitly obeyed than the male chiefs.

Murder when committed by a female is subjected to the same punishment as if committed by a man, in all respects, save in the instance of the killing a husband and in certain cases hereafter to be mentioned. There is no act, committed by a member of the nation which is considered as an offence against the whole body. On the contrary, tho' the nation generally may feel grieved or hurt at the effects of the improper conduct of one of its members, none attempt to avenge an insult or injury except those who are directly affected by it. Nor are there any other acts but murder for which they feel themselves entitled to revenge in the same manner that retaliation is had for a murder. But stealing and adultery sometimes bring death. — Stealing is considered criminal, but not attended by any punishment inflicted by the nation generally. But a thief is always in danger of death at the hands of the person from whom he steals, and if murdered in the maner [under these circumstances] his death is sanctioned by the national customs and not avenged.

Adultery and rape are also considered crimes. The latter is punished only by the contempt of the nation. But an adulterer is subject to the vengeance of the injured husband, and even in case of his death at the hands of one whose bed has been thus violated, the chiefs do not sanction any measure for the punishment of the murderer. These three last are the only acts which are generally detested by the people and liable to punishment

There is no fixed age at which a young man is entitled to all the rights of a man. It depends altogether upon his capacity for business and the possession of property and treatments of a man of business are accorded to some much earlier than to others. Formerly none were permitted to paint with vermillion or other paint but black or in any other manner to assume the practices of men until after the age of sixteen and if characterized by weak minds and want of ambition and energy, this period was extended to seventeen or eighteen.

It is not common for them to assemble for the purpose of deliberation upon questions of internal policy. Each chief has committed to him the care of his particular village and pursues it without let or hindrance from others. On occasions where the general interest of the nation is consulted, such as treaties, wars and the like, and on these only, do the chiefs assemble in council for the purpose of profiting by the views and opinions of the whole.

The nation is divided in five. . . . tribes, having the following names or distinctions, viz:

Mashōakeeau   ⎫
Misheekinārkwau ⎬ or the Little Turtle.
Aseēpun   . . . Raccoon.
Pelāawau   . . . Turkey.
Peewaūpeeau . . The Snow thaws (Munāatwau Snow)
Keelswāu   . . . The Moon.

This division is supposed to have been made for the purpose of government originally, but it cannot be contended, so says the informant, that it is attended with any good effects in these days, when this nation as well as others around have so dwindled away as to be hardly susceptible of division into tribes. — The first & the fourth are supposed to have been originally one. So with the 2nd, third & fifth. Wherefore the first are called Mashōakeeau generally, and the latter Shōngiseeau or those from the air.

MEEĀRMEEAR TRADITIONS

WAR AND ITS INCIDENTS

The question of war is determined by the war chiefs. Oftentimes it is commenced by a single chief, who despatches his Kaūpeeau with a belt of wampum, originally black, but painted red with vermillion, to his brother war chiefs, accompanying his belt with a speech declaratory of his designs. The Kaūpeeau delivers the message and demands the answer, which he returns carefully to his chief, together with note of the time when his ally and young men may be expected at the village. The chief prepares a feast for the occasion of the meeting and when the chiefs have partaken of it they retire and form a compact for the execution of their designs. When this is done they invite the young men to attend a grand council on a day appointed, where an explanation of the motives for the war and the plan for carrying it on, takes place. The young men cannot refuse to accompany their chiefs, and a party is soon organized. The war chief of the Raccoon tribe always commands the party. The Council chiefs are not consulted in the declaration of war, not [nor?] would it be possible for them to prevent it when determined upon by those whose particular duty it is to conduct such expeditions.

It is not uncommon for them to demand redress before declaring war against another nation, and if this is not accorded hostilities are commenced in the most secret manner, without giving to the opposite party any notice of the war.

On the night before setting out the Chiefs and all the young men assemble at the large council house in the village, where each man deposits in a piece of cloth extended for the purpose a piece of *medecine*, being a sign designating the tutelar Deity to whom he commits his life in the expedition about to be undertaken. When each man has deposited something the bundle is tied up and they begin to dance. They dance with little or no cessation all the night and in the morning when they feel themselves ready one of the party, a medecine man, gets up puts the bundle of medecine in to his medecine bag, throws it across his shoulder, commences the war song and leads off. He is followed by the young warriors, who make the air resound with their cries in answer to his song.

The women seperate from the men on the day before they depart for war and are not seen again by them until their return. After a war has been commenced in the manner above described the ceremonies common in the beginning do not take place. Each chief sets out secretly, inviting only the young men of his particular village or family. He dislikes to ask any one of another tribe, because the chief is always considered responsible for his young men, and the debt of his loss would hang over him until another had been killed or taken prisoner in his place. When, however, a young man of another tribe is determined to accompany a chief, he follows his party, at a little distance, and at night when they encamp he seats himself upon his pack at a distance off, but within sight. Perhaps on the second day, but more generally on the third, the war chief when encamped directs one of his men, (his Kaūpeeau) to go and bring the strangers pack. It is done, and the warrior follows it after a small interval, with a slow and measured step. His medicine is added to the general stock in the Waubenaūhkee, or Medecine bag, and he is incorporated with the party.

In marching each man carries his own provisions. Generally in the middle of the afternoon the leader designates the place of encampment and despatches three or four persons to hunt. In the evening they come in to the camp with the game which they have killed. They always march in single file and never pass the carrier of the medicine bag.

When they encamp at night they make their fires to extend from the west to the east. At each end of the fire is a forked stick & upon this rests a pole from which their kettles are suspended. The old men are always encamped upon the south side of the fire, and are called Maamezhōmoalon — or Those who are respected. And the young men are called Maamezhōnoaweeaūnaa, or those who respect. It is considered the particular duty of the young men on the north side of the fire to cook the food for the old men on the south, to furnish them wood, to mend their moccasins & leggins, to bring them water, and minister to every want; in return for which they are looked upon with respect by the nation, and not unfrequently when one distinguishes himself in this manner he is rewarded with the hand of some pretty girl, the daughter of one of the aged men. When marching and encamping it is considered highly improper to step over the fire or to reach any thing from one to another across it.

All authority is vested in the chiefs when going to war. They decide all questions relating to the march and places of encampment as well as the time and place of attack upon the enemy. One of the war chiefs is considered the leader of the party in the march and promulgates the orders which have been previously agreed upon in council with his brother chiefs.

It is customary for them to arrange a plan of operations previous to entering into battle and to appoint certain signals for the government of the warriors in locating themselves and in commencing the attack.

If a party be victorious the warriors return to the village, and when they approach they give notice to their friends by a yell. When they reach the skirts of the town they commence singing the Buffalo dance, and they dance without any intermission to the grand lodge which they surround, continuing the dance for some time, when they enter the lodge in file, following the medicine man, or him who carries the great Waubenauhkee. The dance is continued around the lodge on the inside for about half an hour, when the medecine man suspends the Waubenauhkee from a pole in the middle of the lodge, where it is committed for a short time to the care of two old women, who sit under it and sing, occasionally accompanying their song with shouts. They remain in charge of the Waubenauhkee until night when it is surrendered again to the Paamooseeau (the foremost man) or medicine man who had carried it to war, who takes it to his lodge. During the time that the Waubenauhkee is in charge of the women the warriors are sitting around the lodge, listening to their song.

The subject of the song is thanks to the great spirit for the safe return of those who are assembled in the lodge. It is the duty of the singers to mention each warrior by name in the course of the song. When this is done, he whose name is mentioned arises, and taking up a present of cloth, beads, skins, or whatever else his friends have brot to him for the purpose he carries it to the old women and lays it at their feet. This is done by way of compensation for their services. After this party of the ceremony is accomplished the warriors return to their several homes with their friends and the Paamooseeāū, as before observed, retires with the medecine bag. Five or six days after this, the chief who led the party selects four old medecine men to perform the ceremony of entering the grand lodge with the waubenāūhkee and of comparing it with a duplicate which had been left behind in care of two medecine men of the village. These men go to the lodge of the Paamooseeāū and taking thence the bag, proceed to the grand lodge, preceded by the two who have in charge the duplicate. These latter enter the lodge & place their bag upon a scaffold covered with cloth. In the mean time the other four dance around the lodge four times successively, singing the medecine song. Then they enter the lodge backwards, carrying with them the medecine bag, which they deposit upon the floor. When this is done one of them commences to operate in the way of his profession by emitting from the stomach bones, glass, ice &c, and is followed by the other three; the last of whom swallows all that the others have emitted. This done, they take up the waubenāūhkee and deposit it with its fellow upon the scaffold, when they go through the ceremony of shooting each other with skins of animals, as has been seen. During all this ceremony the young warriors who have returned from war are present. When the four old men last named have finished the ceremonies just described they open the medecine bag which has been carried to war, and nicely arrange the different sacks belonging to the young men, each of whom has deposited something in token of the deity upon whom he placed his fortunes. For this service every warrior makes a small present to the old men, and when all is done every one takes his own sack. When this is done they separate and at night each young man by himself makes a kind of feast at his own wigwam and prays and sings in praises to his diety, and when done, puts away his Kaupēēnawee for another occasion. (It is to be observed that the medecine bag of a single individual is called Kaupēēnawee, but when they are all collected together and placed in the hands of the Paamooseeaū or leader, the bundle or collection is called Waubenaūhkee.)

The meeting of the warriors and medecine men at the distribution of the medecine bags, is attended with a grand feast, preparations for which are made during the interval between their return and the performance of the ceremony. No females are permitted to approach the lodge during the ceremony of distribution.

It is not uncommon for a war party when returning to their village to despatch an express with news of their defeat and the death of young warriors whom they instruct him to name. On such occasions the express enters the village shouting the death yell, and the warriors are met by the friends of those supposed to be dead, mourning their fate. The surprize and joy occasioned by finding the report false and their friends alive are very great, and the deception is considered innocent.

It is customary for a war party to deposit in a secret place, one or two days journey from the place of battle a quantity of provisions and in case of defeat and separation of the warriors this place of deposit is made a rallying point where measures are discussed for a return to the battle or retreat to the village. In case of defeat & return to the village the party enters secretly and disperses to their several homes without any kind of ceremony whatever.

When prisoners are taken they are committed to the disposal of the chief leader, solely. With some of them he chooses to supply the places of young warriors killed in battle, for whose safe return or the return of another in lieu, he is held responsible. Such are painted with vermillion, and arranged in a band by themselves, where they are kindly treated and permitted to march unmolested. Others are doomed to death. These are covered with black paint. When they arrive near the village the prisoners yell is given and the women arrange themselves in two rows from the grand lodge to the path by which the warriors are to enter. Those doomed to death are compelled to run the gauntlet between these rows of women and are often killed before reaching the lodge, but in case any one escapes he or she is surrendered to the man eating society and is thereafter irrecoverable.

In cases when a prisoner does not appear of the proper age or description to supply the place of one who has been killed, and at the same time the chief is desirous to spare his life, he causes him to be presented to some other nation, or to some tribe of his own nation, not concerned in the war. Prisoners of mature age [are] seldom adopted in families. They are either made slaves to a chief or given to the man eating society. The custom of burning prisoners is still in force. Even so late as the last war between Great Britain and the Ustates prisoners were burned by the Shawnees and Miamies.

There is no fixed age at which young men begin to bear arms. It depends altogether upon their strength and capacity to sustain the fatigues of a march. But no young man is permitted to ornament himself with vermillion or to abandon the use of the black paint, until he has accompanied at least one war party. After accomplishing this as a kind of probation, he is received into society and considers himself in all respects a man.

As there is no law regulating the commencement of the time for bearing arms, so on the other hand, no time is fixed when they cease. Every man is guided by his ambition to serve his country so long as his constitution is sufficiently strong to withstand the fatigue of such a mode of life.

Defensive armour is not used. Dependance was formerly

placed upon the bow alone, and this is now transfered to the arms with which they have since been furnished.

Le Gros says that there have been so many reasons for war and some of them so trifling that it would be difficult to state what were the general causes.

It is common for them to fast before setting out on a war party. There are different degrees of fasting. The chief, for instance who takes up the idea in the autumn or winter of going to war in the following spring, paints himself black and fasts at intervals until the time arrives for disclosing his designs to the young men whose company he desires.

The warriors who are to join or have joined a war party, are guided in their fasts by the character of their several manitoos. Those who[se] tutelar deities are the Crow, Hawk &c fast all day, in imitation of those birds. Others fast half a day and others not so much; and the warrior whose manitoo is a wolf does not fast at all, but prides himself upon displaying a ravenous appetite, satisfied with any description of food which he can obtain. He eats from morning till night.

By general custom the wounded are immediately removed from the field of battle, and under the care of two or three persons, are sent to the rallying place of the party, provided the nature of the wounds admits of travelling such a distance. But at any rate they set out for this point, and if mortally wounded, or if the party is defeated and obliged to retreat they are left in the path. If wounded mortally they are seated upon the ground with their faces towards their village.

The Grand father of Le Gros was mortally wounded as was supposed, in battle. He was shot in many places in the breast and his head was litterally hacked to pieces. As the enemy pursued his party closely he directed his attendants to leave him, sitting with his face towards his village, for that he must die at any rate, and they might escape. They obeyed him and fled. In the evening a man appeared to him and stopped the holes or wounds in his body with plates of brass and iron. He recovered and reached his village where he was looked upon as the object of a great miracle. He wore brass bracelets ever after and he could tell by examining these of the death of any one, long before the event happened

It is not customary for women to follow the men to war. But instances have been known where females who have lost all their friends in war have fasted by way of preparation, & having dreamed in their fasts that they were appointed to be the leader of a war party and the bearers of the Waubenāūhkee. In such cases they communicated their dreams to the chiefs, and to them was awarded the honor of carrying the sack & leading the party which was to avenge the death of their friends. They continued to wear the dress of women tho' at the head of the party and generally came off victorious.

When the Miamies had a large village upon the Big Miami the Iroquois attacked them and took a great many prisoners. One of the women who possessed a strong mind and great bravery, assembled the nation and communicated to them that it had been revealed to her in a dream that they were to pursue the enemy and not only recover the prisoners but put every one of their opponents to death. She was habited in nothing but a kind of apron of deer skin dressed black, before & behind, and her flesh was also painted black. The warriors were charmed with her eloquence & appointed her to be the leader of the party. She undertook the task, and after having made all necessary arrangements they sat out. Upon arriving near the Iroquois encampment the spies gave her information of the fact, and she caused every one to pull a piece of spruce or pine from the trees, and with these before them they approached the camp. They fell suddenly upon the sleeping Iroquois and her prediction was literally fulfilled. All the Miamies believe this story in its fullest extent.

They have no tradition of actions fought in canoes. No sieges have been prosecuted by them of which the tradition is still extant. The Chippeways & Pottawatamies once descended from the north upon them at Big Miami at a time when the Miamies had a fort near Piqua. The men were all upon white river, hunting but the place was defended. The women & children who had been left out side of the fort were taken prisoners, but those who remained within sustained the siege until expresses could be despatched to white river and bring relief. When they returned they found that the Chippeways had gone; they followed & overtook them at Fort Meigs where they attacked them in the night and recovered one of their prisoners. The Chippeways fought a short time and then fled, taking the other prisoners along.

PEACE

Ambassadors are sent frequently to negotiate the terms of peace between nations who have been engaged in war. Before their knowledge of the whites the person sent on this occasion carried with him a pole on the end of which was suspended the hinder part of an eagles skin, which is white, together with a grand calumet ornamented with bones and feathers. Across his forehead was painted a streak of blue and the form of a heart was made upon his breast with the same color.

Since the introduction of wampum and flags by the whites the ambassador carries a white flag in one hand and the calumet in the other, accompanied by a belt of white wampum, and wears his usual dress.

He proceeds directly to the principal village of the enemy the chief of which he asks for upon his arrival. He is shown the lodge of this chief and proceeds to it. After setting down his flag at the door he enters and having lighted his pipe and smoked, offers it to the Chief. If he accepts and smokes the sign is held good and the ambassador immediately commences to propose the arrangements for a peace. But if he refuses to smoke at all, it is totally unnecessary to attempt any thing and he makes the best of his way home.

None but village chiefs are entrusted with embassy's of

this kind, and on that account the negotiations are attended with less difficulty than if inferior persons were employed.

An ambassador when on the way to the village of the enemy, is subject to attack and death at the hands of any one who may see him, and feels disposed to prevent a peace. But if he can only reach the confines of the village he is safe. The Chief to whom he is going is held responsible for his body and as well during his stay as upon his return to his own village, his person is considered sacred.

The Ambassador and the other village chief are vested with full power to conclude a peace, and if their negotiations terminate favorably, the chief who has received the application assembles his young men and informs them of the event of the embassy. Then the ambassador returns to his own village where he calls together his young men and makes a similar communication, informing them that the road between the two villages is plain and that all obstructions are removed. After a little time they invite the villagers, their late enemies to come and partake of a grand feast, in commemoration of the cessation of hostilities. At this feast the common dance is the dance of the calumet (Pwaukaūna meēhendgee). It is danced by four persons only. Four grand calumets are laid upon a mat on the ground, ornamented in full with the feathers of the eagle. A pole is placed in the ground near this, and when the dancers are ready to commence, one of the war chiefs marches to the place of deposit, picks up a pipe and striking the pole with the stem, recounts in a loud voice the many feats of bravery which he has performed, and in conclusion says that all those things are smoothed down by the late happy agreement between the contending parties. He then turns about and selecting some active young man he gives him the pipe and desires him to dance. The young man leads off, keeping time to the musick of a drum & gourd which are in the hand of some of the bystanders. He does not dance long before another chief or great warrior goes to the mat and taking another pipe, pursues the same course just described. In this way the pipes are all distributed, and the dancers are occasionally releived by the speech of a warrior who rises, picks up a piece of tobacco or a knife and striking the post therewith recounts his deeds in war.

The guests after returning home reciprocate the compliment and the like ceremonies of feasting, dancing & boasting take place. When this is done the way between the two villages is considered plain & cleared of thorns.

Females, particularly the chiefs, are often instrumental in bringing about a peace, by their efforts to prevent the warriors from carrying into effect their designs for the continuation of hostilities. They are never listened to the first time that a war party sets out, but afterwards they frequently break ground for the village chiefs. Their arguments are directed to the reason and the affections of the warriors. Their appeals are made as mothers and as relatives in a more distant degree of the young men whose lives are about to be exposed. The influence of the women chiefs is very great. They have been known to rush through a crowd of warriors and loose from the stake and lead away an unfortunate prisoner who was suffering the tortures of that mode of death. And instances of this kind are known in which no attempt was made to prevent the execution of their designs.

It is not uncommon for one tribe to act the part of mediators between two others at war with each other. Peace is often effected in this way by the friendly interference of one of the village chiefs of a neutral power, who visits in person the village chiefs of the contending parties and having convinced them of their error & obtained their consent to a peace, returns to his own village and sends his Kaūpeeau to invite the two chiefs to see him. When they arrive their minds being previously prepared by his kind offices he easily persuades them to smoke the pipe of peace, and thus the first steps of a reconcilation are laid. War chiefs have not the power to prevent the making of a peace. They had no flags or armorial bearings before their knowledge of the whites excepting the hinder part of the eagles skin, which was borne upon a pole as before observed by the ambassadors.

DEATH AND ITS INCIDENTS

The customs which prevail in these days differ in some respects from those maintained before their knowledge of the whites. When a person dies the body is washed and dressed in the usual manner but with fine clothing and laid out upon planks or upon the platform in the lodge. It is retained but a short time before interment. If death takes place in the morning the body is interred in the afternoon. If in the afternoon or evening, on the following morning. (Before their knowledge of the whites they seldom clothed the body of a deceased person, but ornamented it with paint & feathers to the highest degree). —

While the corpse is kept in the lodge the relatives & friends of the deceased visit it and sit around it weeping, until the time of its interment.

Four persons, not related to the deceased are appointed by the relatives to carry the body to the grave. This is prepared by digging to the depth of two & a half or three feet, and is lined with planks or bark (or when near the whites the body is put in a coffin.). The corpse is followed to the grave by the near relatives first, who are joined by those more distant and by the friends of the deceased. When they reach the grave the four persons employed in carrying it thither place it in the ground and retire. Then one of the elder relatives approaches and looking at the body, addresses it in language similar to this — "My brother (or my sister,) the master of life has seen fit to determine that you should die. Your body is laid here by the care of your afflicted relatives in the cold earth, but your soul will not remain. That will go to the regions of the west, (the place of the setting sun) to join the vast number of souls which have preceded it. Seek not my brother to take with you any of us, your relatives. We are suffered by the Great spirit to remain here.

MEEĀRMEEAR TRADITIONS 31

We labor only to gain something for the subsistence of ourselves & children and we must, at an appointed time, go to the place where you are now going and where we shall meet. Therefore my brother seek not to take any of us along, as we shall go soon at all events."

After a harangue like this, the breast of the deceased is uncovered and the relatives walk in procession around the grave, each one laying a hand upon the breast of the deceased. When this is done the four carriers approach & cover the body with earth and then two women, previously appointed for the purpose come forward with some food prepared, and the mourners and friends eat of it and depart for home. At twilight one of the near relatives, an old man, or an old woman according to the sex of the deceased, repairs to the grave for the purpose of watching the body. He covers his breast, arms & forehead with earth from the grave and takes his seat upon it. In the course of the night he hears many strange noises, like the howling of wolves, the rushing of wind, the singing of birds &c. This is some medecine man inimical to the deceased, who adopts these noises & forms corresponding with them with a view to approach the body unobserved by the watcher, and to take the tongue or little finger of the deceased as a present to some medecine man, or for his own use as such. If he cannot find the watcher asleep he fails in his attempt. This watcher continues his task four nights successively and if he succeeds in keeping awake all that time, the medecine man dies for his rashness in attempting to disturb the dead; but should he sleep and suffer the approach of the person, his own death, at some day not very far distant is considered inevitable.

Anciently when it was supposed that the death of any person was occasioned by one of the medecine men, or more, who have combined for the purpose, they caused the body to be burned, in order that the persons engaged in conspiring against his life might speedily meet in death, that punishment due to their crime. But this practice of burning deceased bodies has long been exploded. The custom of taking up the bones of deceased persons as it prevailed among the Nauteckoa (Nanticokes) was never known among them.

They often visit the graves of deceased friends. These visits are most frequently made by the females, who occasionally prepare a portion of some choice food and carry it to the grave, at the same time inviting one of the surviving intimates of the deceased to accompany them thither and eat the food, in place of the deceased, who thereby would be equally pleased & profited as if the power of accepting the offering still remained.

Females not related to the deceased are sometimes seen in the place of interment treading around the grave a kind of path. And they often receive presents of small value from the friends of the deceased by way of thanks for their services. Every person is privileged to direct the particular manner in which he shall be interred. If no directions are given they pursue the course already described. But there are instances in which a great fear of death and particularly of interment under the earth, induces some to desire that they may be placed upon the top of the ground in a sitting posture and covered with a kind of frame work of small logs. Others choose that their bodies be placed upon a scaffold in the air, so that if they should rescusitate they might enjoy life without obstruction. It cannot be said however that they generally fear death. The attachment which many have to their children and connexions induces them to regret the decree for their departure, but at the same time they meet the king of terrors with a composure "becoming a man" (as they express it.)

They generally die in the possession of their mental faculties, and commonly take leave of their friends before death. Calling the father & mother brothers & sisters around the dying man says, "My friends, you see that I am going; I see it too, & I have but a word or two to say before leaving you. I leave behind me a wife, whom I love, and I desire that you will treat her with affection and respect for my sake. For my sake too, I hope that you will in case of my death, as soon thereafter as shall be convenient, prepare a dance for me. This will please my soul while on its way to the west. Now I bid you all farewell."

It is to be understood that in mentioning the dance the dying person only chooses the amusement which he was most fond of in life. If hunting or making feasts, he directs a hunt or a feast on his account. And these requests are always complied with on the part of the survivors. Anciently, it was an universal practice to put in the grave of a deceased person some meat and little bark of water, at the feet, and if a man, his rifle or some other thing upon which he set most value. The same custom prevails at this day but to a limited extent. However, it is not uncommon to see large quantities of silver works placed in a grave. In the interment of females the same custom prevails. —

The custom of mourning for the dead was adhered to with the greatest strictness in ancient days. Now, some persons pursue the same customs, rigidly, but the majority do not consider themselves bound by them, but mourn from ten days to as many months, as their inclination prompts them. According to the old custom the husband and wife mourned for each other for the space of two years. The dances of the village were avoided and the survivor went about in a dirty, ill looking dress, painted black in the face and discovering great want of interest in the amusements of the day. At the end of two years the father & mother in law, prepare a proper dress and carry it to the mourner, whom they wash and comb and then dress. If a man, and they have left another daughter, they present her to him in place of his deceased wife, and if a woman and her husband has left an unmarried brother he takes [the] place of the deceased. But at all events the parents in law are obliged by custom to supply the place of the deceased, either from their own families or from others. If the mourner is anxious before the two years expire to terminate the mourning season, he or she, goes to the parents of the deceased and makes them a present of goods or skins. They understand the meaning of this and if they approve of the plan they perform their part as above described.

Brothers, sisters & children mourn only one year. The same disregard to ornament and to the amusements of the society are visible in their persons & conduct. At the end of the year the son, if the deceased be the father, or the daughter, in case of the mothers death, adopts a successor to the deceased. This is attended with a considerable ceremony. To follow the description justly I will give the case of an adoption to supply the place of a warrior. Each man if of any note at all, has his camarade, his particular friend, and this person is chosen by the son to supply the place of his father. As the deceased was fond of war dances and of reciting his feats in battle, the son invites all the young warriors of his acquaintance to come and join in the Discovery dance, (so called from the fact that the dancers imitate all the motions made upon the discovery of an enemy, in creeping, jumping &c &c) —

The young men come to the place prepared, in the night, and they remain there until the dance commences. In the meantime the son despatches a messenger to the intimate of his father whom he intends to adopt, with this message, "I seek you," appointing at the same time a lodge for their meeting. He goes there in the night, the same night appointed for the dance and having stripped the person naked & washed him he leads him into his own lodge where he sees upon a blanket at one side of the room, a complete dress including moccasins & even ornaments, which were the property of his deceased friend, now prepared completely for his use. He is seated by the side of these goods, and soon after he is dressed by a person previously appointed for the purpose. The son then recognizes him as his father, and as by this time the day light begins to approach, he tells him that as his father was fond of joining in the war dances, he had prepared one in honor of his memory; that the young are without and that the drummer, Keehkōōlee paakaumwut, singer, Kaubunēhkongk, moderator and crow are appointed for the dance; and he concludes by demanding as his first act of obedience, permission to celebrate the dance. Consent of course is given, and as the newly adopted father is about to go out of the lodge to witness the dance, a light tap is heard upon the drum, which is succeeded by an universal yell from the dancers. The Moderator gives a sign for the yells to cease and the Crow, (that is a man with a crow skin in his hand) rises and commences to dance. In a few minutes he begins to imitate the actions of an expert spy, now upon his belly, crawling in the grass, and again jumping from one tree to another to avoid discovery or to gain information. At length he comes to the battle. And here of course he was among the most brave. He strikes the post with his crow skin and boasts of the different strokes he has made. When he becomes completely exhausted with fatigue he transfers the crow skin to some other person, who rises and goes thro' a similar dance and historical account. At length all the young men get up and join in the dance, which is now only interrupted by the shout of the moderator at the request of some one who is desirous of describing his achievements in war. This performance is said to be very amusing. When they have danced in this manner for some time, which depends somewhat upon the number who join in it, (or from ten to twelve o'clock in the day) and the warriors have all danced and struck the post, the last dancer surrenders the crow skin to the person adopted as father. This one then follows in the usual manner and when he has finished he dances towards the lodge which he enters entirely naked, except the breech clout. He seats himself by the pile of goods formerly belonging to his deceased friend, and his newly adopted relatives clothe him anew. When he has rested a while he takes each of his relatives by the hand and then departs for his own lodge or village. In leaving the lodge and on the road home he does not on any occasion turn his head to look back. He is accompanied by two men in the capacity of Kaupeeaūkee, who carry the goods which have been presented to him.

He remains always at his own house, but he is nevertheless looked upon as a father by the family which adopted him, and is uniformly treated with great respect by them, as well as depended upon for advice in all matters relating to the family interest. The ceremonies upon the adoption of a mother are similar to those just related, but they are performed altogether by the females, and the feast or dance is such as is customary with them.

It is not customary always to dance or always to feast on these occasions, but that particular amusement or occupation which was most pleasing to the deceased, is followed. So that if the father was particularly fond of shooting at a mark with arrows, or of playing at bowls or the moccasin game, these would take [the] place of the dance. And in cases of dancing, that dance only is known which was most pleasing to the deceased and which he had a right to perform. For a village chief would not be likely to dance the war dances, or a war chief or warrior the trifling dances of the village.

Tho' the person adopted often receives large presents, he does not in the end gain much by it, for it is his duty in the spring following his adoption to make a large present of peltries and dried meat to the family by way of acknowledgement for their choice.

Altho' the father or mother may marry after such adoption, yet the children continue to regard the *adopted* person as the true representative of the deceased parent. Sometimes the adopted & the survivor are joined in marriage.

It has been observed that prisoners of mature age are seldom adopted in families, but this is a mistake. It is not uncommon with this as well as with some other nations, for the chief of a party to present to the children of a warrior killed in battle a prisoner to supply the place of their father. And if such prisoner be pleasing in his appearance he is immediately accepted as a father, married to the mother and thereafter regarded as the head of the family.

This course of adoption has been known to extend to war chiefs. Instances have occurred where the death of a war chief has been avenged by another, who bro.^t to the children a prisoner in his place, and altho' the chieftanship descended to them by law, yet they adopted the person as their father and he was received by the nation & vested with all the powers of the deceased.

This custom prevails among some other nations. The Wyandots at the treaty of St. Mary's had a great chief (village) who was a Cherokee. He was taken prisoner many years ago and adopted in place of a chief who had been killed. If the person thus adopted is supposed to possess the requisite talents for a chief, he is treated with the respect & attention common to his predecessor and his power is not considered any less — They often dispose of the greater part of their property by a nuncupative will — That part which is left without any particular disposition, makes a part of the present to the person who is adopted to supply the place of the deceased.

BIRTH AND ITS INCIDENTS

There is no particular period fixed for naming children, nor its [is it] considered necessary to make any ceremony on the occasion. Very often the parents agree upon a name and the child is known by it thereafter. But more frequently the mother, ten, twenty or more days after the birth of the infant, goes to some old woman of her acquaintance, and having presented her with a small quantity of goods, desires her to come to the lodge and give a name to the child. At an appointed time the old woman goes, and in presence of the family only, takes the child in her arms and commences a kind of harangue, addressed to the infant, in which she describes the circumstances of some fortunate dream which she has had, & concludes by drawing an inference from each particular fact described, applicable to a point in the character of the infant. As, if she saw a deer, he will be swift on foot. If a ferocious animal, he will be a warrior. She argues too that he will be blessed with long life, and she gives him a name descriptive of some one of the circumstances of her dream, taking care however that it is such an one as is usually given to the members of the particular tribe to which the child belongs.

Children never take the name of the father or mother. They never give their children more than one name at a time, but adults frequently change their names. This results from their having been much afflicted with sickness or misfortune which they attribute to something connected with their names, and in such case the person applies to some friend for another name, presenting him at the same time with a small compensation for the service. The name thus given is in presence of a few friends and by them is promulgated to the nation.

They are generally unwilling to tell their names; but it is confidently asserted by those who have passed much time among them, that this is merely the result of a natural diffidence on the subject, common to all Indians.

In addressing each other in the family they are taught to say my brother, uncle, sister &c, and not to use the name of the person spoken to. Indeed it is considered impolite to do so. But in the absence of persons spoken of they are always described by their particular names.

They always address the father & mother in this way, and it is common for them to extend this mark of respect to any aged person with whom they are engaged in conversation. These are the translation of some of their names —

> Kenoazhau — The Pike (a fish) —
> Oamakwau — The Beaver.
> Matshee Kileeartar — The large Beaver.
> Pindgeewau — The Cat Pisheewau.
> Sukeemeear — The Musquitoe.
> Waupelau teekweeau — The yellow head.

Every morning the father of the family rises about daylight and awakes his children by striking upon the bench upon which they sleep & calling out to them to listen to him. He then addresses them in a kind of lecture, setting forth the good & the evil of the world and endeavouring to convince them of the necessity of adhering to the one & of avoiding the other. He draws parralels between the conduct of the good & their consequent happiness and respectability and contrasts these with the many striking instances of bad character which they see.

The Mother adopts much the same course in instructing the female children, and this plan was once very effectual, but it is productive of little good in these days.

They have no person appointed as among some other nations, to instruct the young men in council. The old men however, and particularly the grandfathers are much given to this kind of instruction & are more respected than the younger advisers.

Corporal punishment is very rarely resorted to among them. The parents generally depend upon the effect of advice & persuasion for the accomplishment of their ends. Comparisons have great effect. There is no particular age at which young men cease to be considered as children. It depends altogether upon their disposition and capacity. From seventeen upwards the youth takes upon himself the administration of his own affairs; gets a wife and throws off the shackles of parental government. But anciently the men & the women were considered unfit for marriage until the age of twenty three or twenty five, & they never tho! of breaking the law in this case. It is singular says Le Gros that in these days when the Indians are becoming more & more foolish, they think themselves wise enough at sixteen & seventeen to do things which were formerly prohibited at that age.

In the distribution of property given to the nation, as merchandize at treaties, each child receives the same proportion with the adults. At times however there are small blankets, or small clothes prepared with the others. In such cases these are given to the children in lieu of larger ones. But if there be no choice or difference of this kind the larger articles are equally divided and the parents of the children, take their portions, being considered delegated for that purpose. In the division of their annuities as well as of merchandize the number of souls and not the age or size, are considered. In case of the death of a father & mother the children are dispersed among the different relatives of the deceased & adopted by them. This division is made with a view to lighten the burden of their maintenance and the children are thereafter considered as the particular property of the several persons by whom they were adopted.

Children are considered free and beyond controul of parents when they are married or when they arrive at mature age.

Parental & filial affection were very ardent in ancient days. Then a child was never known to disobey its parent, but in the energetic language of Le Gros, "first his God and then his father" — Now these feelings are weak. Children abuse their parents and very often when intoxicated, beat them; in consequence of which the attachment of parents to their children has greatly decreased. However, it is said that where an instance of sobriety is found among them, that is to say, regular & uninterrupted sobriety, the affection of parents & children towards each other is seen as of old, and continues to the end of life.

Boys & girls are treated with the same affection. If any thing is received as a present and a part is divided among the children great care is taken to treat them all alike in the division. In the death of parents and in case there are no surviving relatives, the children if any are left, are taken by any one or more of the friends of the deceased who feel disposed to compassionate them. No person is compelled to do this, but there is always some one willing to manifest so much respect for the family of the deceased as to adopt the orphans.

There is no sensible difference in the treatment of legitimate and illegitimate children. They are left to the particular charge of the mother, but the father considers it his duty to furnish from time to time, clothing & other articles necessary for the support of the child. And in case of the marriage of a young female after having had a child under these circumstances, the father & mother notwithstanding their separation, both exert themselves for its maintainance.

It is common for the Indian women to have twins, but they seldom have more. The greatest number at one birth, according to the information of my informant is three.

MARRIAGE AND ITS INCIDENTS

There are many customs connected with their courtship, which depend upon circumstances and differ from each other. Generally, when a young man becomes fond of a girl, he reflects upon the nature of his passion and when he has determined to marry her, he goes secretly to the lodge of her parents, in the night, and entering softly, with a small piece of bark by way of a torch light, he gives her a slight shake. She awakes and looks up at him, and upon her answer at that eventful moment depends the result of his attempt. If she is fond of the young man and disposed to marry him she sends him away, with a smile, half consenting at the same time to his stay. Another visit after this finishes the courtship and the female makes room for her lover at her side.

When a young man falls in love with a female whose coldness of manners & pride induce him to feel doubtful of success, he is afraid to commence the courtship. In this case he communicates his passion to his mother, who after waiting a little time for reflection according to their custom, discloses to her husband the attachment of their son. The parents then collect a parcel of goods and skins for a present and they set out for the lodge of the young female. The old woman travels in front with the bundle upon her back followed by her husband. When they have arrived at the lodge they enter, the load is deposited, the father and mother of the girl sought for, and when they come the father of the lover addresses them telling them that "they have come to bring them fire, water & moccasins". By this figurative expression, which alludes to the labours of the son in law during the advanced age of the parents of his wife, they understand the meaning of the visit. The suitors return home, and after their departure the parents of the girl call her into their presence & disclose the cause of the visit, soliciting her at the same time to have pity upon them & provide by her own marriage for their comfort in old age. When the girl has consented the parents dress her out in all the finery they can muster and set out for the lodge of the young mans parents, the father walking before, the daughter next and the mother in the rear. Upon arriving at the lodge they enter in the order of march and the girl being seated the father commences a kind of speech to the parents of the son, thanking them for the compliment paid them in choosing their daughter as well as for the present made on that account. They give the daughter a lecture upon her duty to her husband & concluding with pointing to the platform in the lodge and saying "there is your bed, see that you do not defile it", they return to their own lodge.

When a young man performs the courtship himself as has been mentioned firstly, he sets up in the lodge of his mistress until the father awakes, and then he rises to depart, leaving behind him his blanket or something else as a proof that he did not come with a design to sport with the girl, but with serious intention to marry her. Then he goes out to hunt, and if he is so fortunate as to kill a deer or any large game, he does not go to his own lodge, but carries it to the lodge of his mistress, where he sometimes drops it at the door & passes on without speaking & at others goes in & leaves his rifle in further proof that he is disposed to join the family.

A short time after the young people are married the husband presents to his wife a horse newly saddled & bridled, a new rifle or some other valuable present, without directing her how to dispose of it. She sets out, & if a horse is the present she leads him by the bridle, to her fathers house, and when her brothers are all assembled she informs her eldest brother of the kindness of her husband in making her such a grand present and concludes by offering it for his acceptance.

He accepts it & she returns to her own family. In the hunting season following the brother preserves all the fattest meat, which he dries carefully, and in the spring when he returns to his fathers house he invites the assistance of his young friends and they carry the meat to the lodge of his brother in law where he presents it to his sister in return for the horse. She gives it to her mother in law, who calls together all the members of the family & distributing the present among them informs them of the industry & kindness of the hunter in collecting so much game & presenting it so freely. The old women, in return for this gift, direct the assistance of the young females & having collected together large quantities of vegetables & sweet roots, such as are usually cultivated or gathered by the women, they transport it all to the lodge of the last donor.

This last ceremony ends the reciprocal gifts between the parties or in other words, the honey moon is over, and the newly married couple begin to find the business of life serious & requiring attention. So they live for themselves thereafter.

An Indian is allowed to have as many wives as he can maintain. My informant has had four, but he has never known more than five in the same family. The first wife, or she who is first married, is considered superior to all the others. She is the head of the family in fact, and nothing is projected or executed by the others without first having consulted her. The husband is careful to show the same attention, (if not more) to the eldest wife as to the youngest, and in the division of presents or property each has an equal part. They compose the same family, residing in the same lodge but each has her particular bed, to which the husband resorts at pleasure, generally however endeavouring to prevent jealousy by lying with them alternately. They sometimes become jealous of each other and when the husband is absent they quarrel, and sometimes fight, but in his presence they maintain good order & rule and conceal from him any feeling which may draw down his resentment. When a man loses his wife her surviving sister, if she leaves any, is considered at the disposal of the husband, who may marry her if he chooses, and he generally does so; but if she wishes to unite with another & he consents it is all well, and she does so.

Adultery is considered criminal as well in the man as in the woman. And it not unfrequently happens that the husband of the women caught in adulterous intercourse punishes the offence by killing his wife or the man who is found with her, as he esteems the one or the other most guilty. In this case the murder does not come within the general rules, but on account of the enormity of the offence forms an exception, and the act is not avenged, either by the friends of the wife or of her paramour.

There is no law of divorce. The husband abandons or turns away his wife or the wife leaves the husband, for any cause which seems to justify to themselves the course. The ill conduct of the wife and the cruelty of the husband are however the most frequent causes. Sometimes the wife is possessed of too much spirit to brook the abuses of her husband & takes it upon herself to punish him; and if in any attempt of this kind she kills him, his death passes unavenged. — In the event of a divorce the wife generally takes the children under her care, tho' the law on the subject is that they shall be equally divided. In the event however of their being taken by the mother, the father affords his aid from time to time for their support, in the same manner as he would have done had the divorce not taken place.

Le Gros once knew a woman to have two husbands at the same time and to live with them both happily. The men occupied different lodges and the wife visited them alternately. The arrangement was made in consequence of the wife having fallen in love with the second husband and being so honest as to disclose the fact to her first one, who was so pleased with the candour exhibited by her that he consented to the connexion. They each had children by her who were kept together under the charge of the wife, and were clothed by the joint labours of the husbands. —

If a man marries a widow who has one or more daughters

and after living with her sometime becomes attached to the daughters or one of them, he applies to his wife for her assistance in procuring the consent of the daughter to a marriage. The wife, if she loves her husband & is desirous to please him undertakes the task and does not fail to accomplish it. Instances occur too where a man marries at the *same time* the mother and the daughter.

Marriage is prohibited with uncles or aunts, nephews or neices and first couzins Second couzins may marry, but it is less common, even in this degree than among parties not related to each other.

They do not serve any time for a wife; but often when a young man wishes to cultivate the good will of the friends of the female, he gives to one of her brothers a present of skins or goods, which opens the way to an intimacy between them and in process of time he so far gains the good will of the brother as to interest him in his behalf and obtain his services with the sister. This is but one of the many different plans which they have for obtaining a footing in the affections of the family. Sometimes a long course of attention to the parents is rewarded with the hand of their daughter. This occurs particularly in war. Le Gros's first wife was presented to him by his superior chief in consequence of his attention and respect to the chief during a warlike excursion. He could not have refused the offer if he had been so inclined; but as it happened he felt anxious to marry the young female before he had thought of the plan by which he was to obtain her hand.

As the fact of living together and cohabiting, constitutes marriage among them, it is, consequently, impossible for a man & woman to live together without being married.

Individuals of either sex do not often live to an advanced age without being married. There are however, instances like the following. A man and a woman agree to cohabit with each other for life and to avoid if possible begetting any children. They live at the lodges of their friends and have no intercourse but at night, or at convenient seasons during the day.

They use every precaution to prevent their conduct from gaining publicity & the man frequently rewards his mistress with presents. But if unfortunately the woman becomes pregnant the father acknowledges the child and contributes from time to time to its support. They sometimes pass their lives in this manner, without ever living in the same lodge or making a publick acknowledgement of the fact of cohabitation, neither party proving faithless to the other. This is considered disreputable to the parties, and when for the circumstance just mentioned or any other, their conduct becomes known, the parents use their exertions to bring about a connection between them according to the customs of the nation.

In these days it is common for unmarried women to have children. Their reputation is not materially affected by it, and in some instances not at all

It is supposed that one third of the Indian women never have any children. Among those who have them, about six may be considered the average number in a family. There are some families that have 13. The average interval between their birth is supposed to be eighteen months. The women commence child bearing at the age of eighteen and do not cease always until they reach fifty.

FAMILY GOVERNMENT &C

The husband is a complete lord. He rises in the morning, takes his gun and goes to visit his traps. If he finds any game he brings it to his lodge and throws it down at the door, when his trouble with it is ended. Almost the only assistance which he renders to his wife is in the planting and hoeing the corn, and, when going to the hunting ground to make a couple of forks and a pole for the kettle to be suspended by.

The woman is obliged to take the axe and cut wood, carry it to the lodge, make fires, cook the food, sweep the lodge and make mats. It devolves upon her to gather & put away the corn & vegetables, to dress all the game & skins which her husband brings in, and to examine his moccasins and leggins and repair them every day, if necessary. When going to their hunting ground the husband leaves her as soon as he has prepared a place for the kettle and while he is engaged in hunting she collects poles & bark and makes a lodge. If necessary to remove the camp she must do it, unless in cases where there is too much baggage for her to manage, when she received occasional assistance from the husband. When however the husband advances in years, he feels less proud and gradually wears into the habit of assisting his wife in the discharge of many of her domestic duties. So that among the old people they often see a man cutting wood, dressing meat and making fires. But during the vigorous season of youth, the warrior or hunter feels it a disgrace to perform any manual labour whatever.

Anciently it was uncommon for a man to quarrel with his wife or to correct or punish her in any manner, but since the introduction of liquor among them they have degenerated, and now nothing is more common, particularly when they are drunk, to abuse & sometimes beat their wives.

They are particularly careful to appear cold & reserved before strangers towards their wives; and any fondling or playfulness is considered a proof of weakness of mind.

If a man should murder his wife for any cause but adultery he would be liable to punishment from her friends as in other cases of murder. But under *this* circumstance if he kills her, he has only to go to her parents, with a present of goods, and explain & prove to them her intercourse with the man whose crime occasioned her death, and the matter is settled at once. And even in case of her death for any other improper conduct than that just mentioned, if it is at all avenged, it must be done by some other relative than her brothers, who decline any interference.

The government of the family is committed to the father, but during his absence it is transferred to the mother, whose duty it is however, on all occasions, to correct and advise the females.

The Indian women are supposed to be as much addicted

to scolding as the whites. The husbands seldom interfere to prevent them, or indeed to take any notice of them at all, and they become at length ashamed of themselves and stop.

Instances sometimes occur in which the husband becomes a drunken or a lazy, worthless fellow and the whole care and management of the domestic concerns devolves upon the wife; and it is said that they frequently succeed in the discharge of this duty as well as the men of other families do. —

MEDECINE

Most of their diseases are produced by a redundance of bile. The Rheumatism too, is very prevalent, owing to their frequent exposure in the chase. The most common medecines are emetics, which they administer in all cases resulting from the overflow of the biliary ducts. These are composed of roots, which are pounded & mixed in warm water. In cases of head ache, of weakness or heaviness in the eyes and often in case of a general lassitude of the system, bleeding is resorted to. This is sometimes performed in the arm, and at others in the head or foot. They bleed with a piece of flint, which is fastened in the end of a stick and inserted into the vein by means of a sudden blow from another stick. There are persons who are considered expert in performing this operation, but patients frequently bleed themselves, in which case they construct the stick containing the flint so long as to reach to the hand, in which it is held, while with the other hand the blow is given.

They are not so expert in curing the rheumatism as in other diseases. Some persons have laboured under the disease for years. Their usual treatment is to pound some roots & weeds and apply them with a bandage, to the parts affected.

There are many roots & weeds used by them for emetics, the most common of which is the root of the Buckeye.

They often count the pulsation of the arteries, to know the state of the disease.

The consumption is not uncommon among them, and is seldom cured. This & the rheumatism are the only chronick diseases excepting *poison*. Strange as it may seem, they attribute many of their deaths to the malign influence of a medecine man, who had some trifling private animosity against the deceased. And they generally account in this manner for the termination of incurable diseases, saying that any attempt to remove them would have been worse than useless and that all their labour might have been saved if they could have known the nature of the disease. However there is in the possession of the medecine men, or among the most expert of them the same root used to convey the disease, and this, this alone, can effect a cure. The possessors of this remedy never undertake the task of removing the disease, without a handsome fee, in shape of a horse, a bundle of goods, a rifle, or something of the kind.

The poison is supposed to be given in the food of the person, or in a dram of whiskey, prepared for him.

None but the principal medecine men know how to dig for this root; and even themselves are put to much trouble in finding it. It has a vine growing from it, which is scarcely perceptible, and which extends over the surface of the earth to a great distance. Very often when a medecine man has discovered the vine, he is obliged to travel two or three days before he reaches its source. Upon accomplishing this he leaves a mark & returns to his village, where he prepares a sacrifice, consisting of a kettle, eight pieces of tobacco and eight articles of merchandise. These he transports to a spot near the root and there deposits them, when he is permitted to dig the medecine & return, leaving his sacrifice to the mercy of the wind and rain. The medecine administered to relieve persons afflicted as above described, is given just as in ordinary cases, but in a more secret manner.

The person procuring the root with a view to its use as a poison is limited according to the extent of the sacrifice. If he sacrifices four pieces the root which he procures operates to kill two persons, if six pieces, four persons; and if eleven pieces, which is the greatest number, his power lasts many years. At length, when his medecine is all gone & with it his power of using it, he begins himself to dwindle away and is often, together with his whole family the subject of a like attack from some other of his profession.

ASTRONOMY &C

The year is divided into two seasons.

Naāpeenweēk — Summer.
Peepoanweē — Winter.
 and also into moons — viz:

Tshetshākoa — Crane —— May. (because in that moon the Cranes are seen flying over. They add *Keels wau* or *moon*, when necessary to the sense, but it is not common.)
Oakōaweear — Whipoorwill. June — for same reason.
Utshetsheēkutaa — Hilling corn moon — July. (from Utsheketōmingk — to Hill (Corn))
Keēshingwaa — Fit to be eaten — August. In this moon the corn is fit to eat.
Misheēweear — Elk — September. In this moon the Elk run. It is said to be very easy to kill them in this moon, by imitating the noise which they make & thereby attracting them.
Saushekūoalyāī — The moon of the narrow fire. October. In this moon the leaves are yet green and the fire being put to them does not spread but runs in a narrow & limited space.

These are the Summer moons.
Those of Winter are —

Keeyōoleeär — Running moon — for Deer — Novem.
Yaupensāu — Young Buck moon — The bucks two years old, run in this moon — Dec.
Iiyāupeear — Buck moon — In this moon the Bucks drop their horns. Jan.
Mukwāu — Bear moon — In this moon they have young. Feb.
Muhkōanse — Cub moon — Those of 2 years can have young in this moon. [March]
Ōntekwe — Raven moon — April — The sap runs in this moon & the ravens are most numerous.

They have no ceremony upon the appearance of the new moon. I have found them disposed to avoid the expression of any opinion, as possessed by themselves or the nation on the subject of the heavenly bodies, or the size & formation of the earth. This may be the result of a consciousness that they must have erroneous ideas on the subject, but they alledge that they have never endeavoured to form an opinion.

The meteors which we call shooting stars are said to be Indians who are courting. — In ancient days, there were two young females lying together engaged in conversation. It was a fine evening and the stars shone brilliantly. Above their heads they saw a very large red looking star and another, its companion, or nearest neighbour, of a smaller size. One of the females observed that she would like to have the red star for her husband, and the other replied that the small one would suit *her* taste. During the night two men approached, & awoke them, telling them they were the stars for which they had wished, and they laid themselves down. The young women were much pleased, but what was their astonishment, when awaking at day break, he who had passed himself as the large red star, was found to be a wrinkled old man, & the other a fine, handsome youth, and particularly when both suddenly vanished from their sight and were not seen [any] more.

RELIGION

They entertain no doubt of a future state of rewards and punishments, correspondent to their good or evil conduct in this life. According to the opinion generally entertained, there are different kinds of punishment for those who have been wicked here below. The soul of the deceased after death, sets out to travel to the regions of the west. If the individual has led a good life and deserves the favours of the great spirit he is transported to a place where the souls of deceased persons enjoy an eternity of bliss.

Their ideas upon this subject will be best explained by relating the origin of their belief, which will show as well the mode of reward as of punishment.

Many, very many ages ago, a young Miami died. His relatives and friends assembled around the corpse and wept his loss. He was dressed and laid out in the manner common in those days, with his bow and arrows at his side. They were then in the habit of keeping the body of the deceased some days before interment, and that was the case with this one. Some time before the funeral was to have taken place his relatives discovered signs of returning life. They watched the body carefully and not long after, the young man awoke and spoke to the bystanders. Their tears were changed to tears of joy. They gave him some water to refresh him and desired to know what he had seen & felt during his absence from them. He promised to gratify them and commenced his story in the following words.

"I thought that I was dead and that having left all my relations here, I sat out, travelling to the west. The trail was very large and bore evident marks of having been travelled a great deal. I travelled some time, when I arrived [at] a place where the roads forked, and I saw at the forks of the path an old man, who told me that one of these roads led to a house where a large fire was kept up for the purpose of punishing by burning, all those who had been guilty of heinous offences on earth, such as murder, stealing, adultery &c. I concluded that this was not my road and I chose the other and continued travelling on. Not long after I passed a large lodge, at the door of which stood an immense dog. I was told that this dog was stationed there for the purpose of devouring all such as had been distinguished for their cruelty to animals, particularly to those of his own species. As I had not been guilty of this offence I passed on. At some distance from this lodge I came to a deep and very rapid river. It was too deep for me to wade and to rapid to attempt swimming it, but there were two large trees laying in the water, which had fallen from opposite banks & touched each other. Upon these I ventured to cross. I reached the opposite shore in safety, and upon the bank I found an old man. I enquired his business there and he told me that it was to show travellers the road, as it had become difficult to pursue it, so few persons passed. He directed me how to proceed and continuing my route I arrived at a lodge, where I saw another old man at the door, holding in his hand a wooden bowl and the usual number of plumb stones. He asked me to play at Sansawīngee, but I declined and passing this lodge I continued to travel on, and soon met two men, standing on opposite sides of the road, each of them holding in his hand a Pekitehōmingk (stick used in playing ball sometimes called Pekitarhunār;). They asked me to join them but I would not. I next arrived at a place prepared for dancing. I saw there four old men, employed as singers. They demanded whence I came & upon being informed they pointed out to me many of my relatives in the dance and asked me to join them, as they were abundantly supplied with every thing necessary to eat and to wear. I was about to join my friends, when I recollected that I had left my bow on the road, and I thought I would return and procure it. I accordingly sat out and pursued the homeward track, often meeting persons on their way to one or other of the places allotted to them. At length I came to where I had left my bow and I saw it enveloped in a flame of fire. One end only protruded itself from the flame, and I attempted to catch hold of this; in doing which I awoke and am as you see me."

Upon this vision they rest their belief of a future state — They have among them a spice of the Pythagorean creed, for it is said that when the deceased is a parent, and his children do not adopt another in his place, as has been described, the soul remains upon the earth, in the body of an owl or some unclean animal and haunts the family of the deceased.

They do not universally believe in the existence of a Supreme and ordinary deities, as do the other Indians. At least Le Gros appears to be somewhat sceptical on this subject. He says "There may be such things as a great spirit and a Bad spirit, and they may not be. You are not certain of either, nor am I." —

Their belief in ghosts is implicit. When the surviving

friends of a deceased person do not pay proper attention to his memory, in making a dance, a shooting match or a feast for him, agreeably to his taste while living, as has been before mentioned, the anger of the ghost becomes roused and he visits them to remind them of their duty. Some one will feel a slight sensation of the ear & hear a kind of singing sound, or will have a tremulous motion of some of the nerves of the arm or leg, the first of which indicates the speaking of the ghost and the latter the touch. Being thus reminded the relatives prepare to perform the necessary sacrifice to the memory of the departed. They procure some fine meat and having prepared a feast in the family they partake of it, at the same time throwing a portion in the *edge* of the fire, *so that the ghost may not burn his fingers;* or if he was fond of whiskey they sprinkle a small quantity on the ground near the fire for the same purpose; or they make a dance — In the night after doing this the ghost comes to the lodge to get his share, at which time some one of the family to whom the deceased was attached during his life, is permitted to have a *coup d'oeil* of his figure. There was an old man at the old Miami village at Fort Wayne, who was peculiarly favored with these nocturnal visits. He often had warning & ordered his wife to prepare a kettle of food which he caused to be suspended in the lodge, together with a sufficient number of spoons. In the morning after he would send for another old man, to whom he gave the food, as the ghosts satisfied their appetites always, without taking away any of the contents of the kettle.

Some of the most perfect among their medecine men are supposed to be wizzards. Such are those of whom they speak of as possessing the power to poison persons or cure them of a disease originating in poison. They are sometimes consulted in cases of extreme sickness, when they unite their knowledge of simples to the power which they possess as wizzards (Mehtshĭngweea). The doctor examines the patient with the eyes of an eagle, a wood pecker or some other winged fowl which he has borrowed for the occasion, and after repeating some short sentences in a murmur and striking his own breast, he vomits up a small whitish substance which he holds in the palm of his hand and examines attentively. He tells the patient that this will decide his fate. If it works thro' his hand he will die, but if it remain upon the hand he will recover. Then giving him a small supply of roots and encouraging him to have good faith, he leaves him. After a short time he returns to visit his patient and then tells him how he is to fare. He probably draws his conclusions from the state of the sick man at the time of his visit.

These men have the power to injure persons at a great distance from them. Sometimes if one of them has an antipathy against another person, no matter how far off, he will resolve that that person shall die. He then takes a small piece of charcoal together with a little wool from his blanket, and rubbing these together a short time he forms a fly, a hair, or some other thing which he blows into the air and bids it to go. When this fly arrives at the destined point, it strikes the victim, upon one of his legs, perhaps at the knee; a smart pain is soon after felt, the person complains, goes to bed, rises in the morning much stiffened, continues to grow worse, and the pain increasing & extending upwards to the vitals, in four or more days, as has been resolved by the wizzard, he dies. — There is no remedy whatever for attacks of this kind.

At other times one of these men will take a liking to the horse, rifle, or silver ornaments of a young man — He prepares one of his little messengers and attacks him — The young man grows sick. His friends mourn. The old doctor hears of his sickness from some villager and advises that some one be applied to for his cure. The friends are told of this and as the doctor is always ready, they send to employ him, at the same time making him a handsome present of the property of the patient, perhaps the same article which he wanted. The doctor comes — He feels the limbs & body of the patient at the seat of pain, & perhaps squeezes out something from the flesh. He strikes or rubs him upon the breast and the patient vomits. All these things the doctor swallows, and when he has done he takes his present & departs, pronouncing his patient recovered.

There is no religious society, of any description among them, nor any persons who officiate in the character of priests. —

When they pray for favor or assistance their prayers are addressed to their tutelar deities and not to the Great spirit. Every man has his particular guardian god. When young he is taught to fast for a whole winter, nay, oftentimes six months. He rises very early in the morning, blacks himself and goes out to hunt or to play, without eating. At first he fasts until noon, and at length until night. He continues fasting, until he has a vision, in which he is permitted to see his god, in the form of a man with his bow, a woman with her hoe, a tree &c —

If destined to be a warrior, the man presents to the dreamer a piece of flesh, saying, "You shall eat of this meat four times" meaning, "You shall go to war four times" — They have the greatest faith in the events foretold in this vision and by their own exertions they often take place.

When they pass an uncommon rock, or mountain or enter a cave, they are in the habit of depositing pieces of tobacco, as an offering to the deity which inhabits them. It is not an uncommon thing for an Indian to lay upon a large stone a quantity of tobacco, and then to address it — "O Stone, you are fond of tobacco & I here give you a little to smoke — I am fond of life, I like to stay in this world and I hope you will let me remain, and that you will give me success in hunting and in travelling." —

When crossing a dangerous place in the lake, or when the wind blows they throw some tobacco in the water, (to appease Neptune I suppose,) to insure a safe passage.

They have no ideas respecting a final judgement.

GENERAL MANNERS &C

When two Indians meet they shake hands. They do not always enter into conversation, particularly the young men, who often separate without making any enquiries. But the usual observations, when two have not seen each other for some time, are — "I am glad — I thank the Great spirit, that he has permitted us to meet. Whence do you come? Where are you going?" — Sometimes after these preliminaries they make mutual enquiries about their families. —

When a man has been long absent from home on a journey or in hunting, and returns to his village, he enters his lodge without any ceremony and seats himself upon the bench or scaffold. He caresses his children chats with his wife and in other respects manifests his pleasure at being able to return. There is no uncommon coldness or formality evinced in his conduct, as is said to be the case among some nations. — On the other hand, the Indian in this case as when he is in love, conceals from the persons present any strong excitement or feeling of affection towards the object of his passion.

They have no words equivalent to our habit of swearing, but they often make use of obscene language in their games & dances. —

Much respect is paid to age. The youth are taught the necessity of it, from their infancy. Often the young men take to the aged the finest part of a deer which they have killed, or a skin, some tobacco, or moccasins. Their reward for this good conduct is found in the praises of the villagers, who are carefully made acquainted with all the facts of the kind which transpire.

The old men often take it upon themselves to advise the young, either singly, or when they are assembled together at play: but there is no particular manner of doing this, nor is it considered incumbent upon them to do so.

They often meet in the long winter evenings to amuse each other by the relations of tales of fiction, calculated to interest the hearer & drive away ennui. This task is generally committed to one of the oldest men and if any one of them is renowned as a story teller, he is followed by a crowd of young men every evening when he goes out to visit. —

Their course in an unknown country is regulated by the moss upon the trees, by the general course of the streams and their size and by the sun.

Each nation is supposed to have a manner of preparing their encampment, peculiar to itself, and altho' the general resemblance is so great that to the eye of a stranger no difference is perceptible, yet an Indian can readily distinguish the nation & tribe to which an encampment belonged. The Miamies, for instance are vary careful in the construction of their camp or lodge, and at the side of each man a forked stick is thrust into the ground from which his horn & his moccasins are suspended. — They build their fire between two short logs, which are placed endwise to each other — On the contrary, the other nations build their fire of long pieces of wood & none are so careful as to provide a forked pole for their moccasins. The number of persons at an encampment is known by the marks of their bodies upon the ground, and the particular tribe & the course which they travelled when leaving the camp are known by marks on a tree near by. —

They spare the lives of snakes of every description. — And they give for a reason the following story. In the early days, there was a little boy, who had lost his father and mother. He was then in the fasting season, and often went out to kill small birds with his bow. He found it difficult to obtain enough of these for his subsistence. One day he was going along, having killed a few birds, when he was addressed in the voice of a man. The man desired to know if he had killed some birds, to which he answered in the affirmative. Well, said the man, you may hereafter be permitted to kill deer, Bears, raccoons &c, and live as other people do. The boy was delighted, and wondering who could be speaking to him he looked up, and he beheld the speaker in a large black snake, winding himself around a tree.

GAMES, DANCES & AMUSEMENTS

The Shaūwonoa Kūnkee naāmingh — or The dance in Shawnee was borrowed from that nation upon their first meeting, at Piqua, many years ago. It is danced for amusement merely, and on account of being very much admired it is in use very generally at the adoption of a person to supply the place of one deceased, as very few die, who do not prefer it to all other dances. It is danced at night, a feast having been prepared to eat upon finishing it. The leader of the dance is followed at a distance by the person to be adopted, who at a similar distance is followed by a female & she is followed by a male, who in his turn is followed by another female & so on to complete the ring all but the leader & the adopted person being in close order. They dance around a fire in a ring, following their leader. The musick consists of a drum, accompanied by the voices of one or two good singers seated upon the ground, or by that of the leader of the dance. When the dancers are fatigued they seat themselves & rest, until some other person jumps up & begins to dance.

Tshiswaānarkee, is a dance common to the nation and originating among them. It is danced much like the one just described and differs from it only in this, that there are two rows of dancers around the fire instead of one, and that all persons, old & young, even men so decrepid as to be compelled to use a stick for support, join in the dance. It is in use only after the death of a person. One year from the time of his death the surviving relatives send out and procure a young or half grown buck, of which they make a feast. When every thing is prepared they invite all the relatives and friends of the deceased to attend. They commence the dance early in the evening and continue it with little intermission until the following morning, being furnished at intervals during the night, with food from the kettles, by two servants or cooks, who are paid for their services by the relatives of the deceased. The musick used consists of two drums, which are beaten by two old men, who accompany them with their voices. No other ceremony accompanies the dance. At daybreak or soon after they disperse & return to their several homes.

Olaanāuzwaunaukee, the Buffalo dance — This is danced only by the warriors after their return from battle. On the day that they enter the village, they bring their prisoners near the lodge where the grand medecine bag is deposited and there they dance, to the musick of a gourd & song only. They have no fire, but they dance around in a kind of ring, the leader being very much stooped. If they have no prisoners, they dance nevertheless, for the scalps which they have taken. These are suspended from a pole near the medecine bag. The women and the villagers are excluded from this dance, tho' they may always assemble to look on. Four days after the return of the war party, a large feast is prepared, to which the warriors invite all the villagers about, and then this dance is again gone thro' with. They dance it only in the day time, commencing in the morning & ending at sunset. No speeches are used, nor striking of the flag staff or allusions to their feats in war. This dance is said to have originated among themselves.

Māandwingee — "Let us beg" The Begging dance, is also common among them. This dance needs no description, being alike among all nations.

These and the dances incidentally described heretofore are said to be all they have.

Among their games they have the Sansawīngee — or Bowls. With a wooden bowl and six plumb stones one side of which is black & the other white, they amuse themselves for days together. And they frequently lose all they have upon the event of it, sometimes betting their horses or guns. As the game is played among the Miamies the player counts nothing unless he turns up five at least of the whole number, of the same color. This counts him half of the amount bet, and six of the same colour wins it. They often bet so high & lose so much that quarreling & bloodshed are the consequences of this game, simple as it is. —

moccasin   use it   game

Mūkisinee aayōangee mekindingk — The Moccasin game is a game upon which also they hazard much. It is played by four or more persons and sometimes by two. When a number are playing they divide themselves into two parties. Four moccasins are used. They are placed in a row between the competitors. One of them commences the game by putting secretly into one of the moccasins, a small bullet or a grain of shot. He then takes his seat and one of the opposite party rises and takes up or strikes the moccasin which he supposes to contain the ball. If he touches the right one he gains a point and it is his turn to hide the ball for the opposite party, but if he miss the moccasin he loses a point & takes his seat, when the moccasin is moved or the ball rehid. Each time that one wins he gains one of four small sticks or counters and each time that he loses, the opposite party take one of them; and when either party gets the whole of the four sticks the game is ended and the articles staked upon it are delivered to the winners. When a large party is collected to play this game they frequently paint themselves about the eyes, both above & below them, because they say that the game was first taught them by a man whose name was Mindēekwau or the Owl.

Shoakwauwulaokāunee, The Rolling game — is much like the game of nine pins. A place upon the ground is made smooth and at the distance of fifty short paces nine pins are placed upon their ends, near together. The Ball is much of the size which we use, and to enable the player to guide it & to throw it with the greater velocity, holes are made in it for the fingers and thumb. Five pins being down, counts three, and if the one in the middle and no other is thrown down, the game is won; that is ten. —

Paapāashulaawunār — The definition of this word I cannot learn. But it is the name of a game in which the bow & arrow is used. The exercise consists merely of shooting at a mark for money or skins and there is no particular rules of game. —

Paapaamootekutaūwee — is another game of shooting. They form a small ball of bark and throw it into the air, and as it come down they shoot at it with the arrow. They generally hit it. Large bets are however made upon the game and when once interested they spend much time in it. —

Maamaaskaukutaūwee — is also played with the bow. It is merely a trial of strength to see who can shoot farthest, and he whose arrow is in the rear forfeits a sum previously agreed upon.

Pekitarhunār Pukwaūhkoan — The Indian game of ball, is too well known to need a description. The only thing in which the Miamies appear to differ from other nations is in the use of a wooden ball, perforated with two holes, so as to make a singing noise when going thro' the air.

This game used to be played by many persons at the same time. Le Gros has seen five or six hundred engaged at once. It was always considered a dangerous game, on account of the force with which they throw the ball. Many persons have been wounded & some killed by it, but no accident of this kind stopped the play. On the contrary little or no notice was taken of persons who were hurt, the players devoting rather, all their attention to get the ball to the goal of their party. — The players are entirely naked excepting the breech clout. Four long poles are arranged on one side of the playing ground, upon which all parties laying wagers, deposit or rather hang the articles at stake. The winners go to the poles and select the different deposits and seperate. They often play a long time before deciding the game. Sometimes when the players are expert and numerous, a whole day is employed in playing one game. —

       Paper   game

Mausunaukaūnee mekindingk — Cards — at cards they play all fours and loo, and they have another game resembling in the manner of betting the french game of *vingt et un*, but the cards counts as in other games and the tricks decide it, whereas in *vingt et un* the number of spots decide the game.

They are fond of wrestling & swimming, but of late years they practice it much less than formerly.

They never heard of a game in which an Indian jumped from hole to hole, suffering others to fire at him as he jumps. —

Marmeeshauhkwauhenar — is another game much in use among them. A flat, circular piece of brass or tin is suspended from a very tall pole, by a string, and the players endeavour to hit it by throwing a small wooden ball from a peketarhunār, or stick such as generally used in playing ball. The number of the game is agreed upon between the players and each time that one of them hits the Marmeeshauhkwaukaūnee or piece of tin he counts one or more, as has been previously agreed upon.

Shoakwauhkeenaū Shingaukekaūnekee — This game is played upon the ice. A bow, about fifteen feet long, four inches wide and half an inch thick is prepared of hickory or other tough wood. It may be said to resemble a sleigh runner rather than a bow, in shape, and one end is thicker & heavier than the other. Two persons only, play at a time, they set up stakes or bounds, at a considerable distance apart and starting at an intermediate point, each endeavours to gain his own boundary by throwing the bow towards it. The other in the mean time is ready to meet it & throw it back, and the game is decided by the accomplishment of the task to reach the stake. Altho' only two persons play at a time, the whole village are often engaged as spectators & betters. And challenges are often sent by one village to another, the messenger bearing by way of invitation a miniature bow, ornamented with the articles proposed to be staked upon the issue of the game. This he delivers to those in the opposite village who accept the challenge by returning another messenger with a similar Shingaukekaūne or bow and appointing a time & place for meeting. Poles are arranged upon the ground for the purpose of suspending the articles which the different villagers choose to bet upon the issue of the game.

They often dream in early life that they are to excel in

some one of these games, and by much practice & attention they occasion a verificcation of their visions.

Le Gros recollects a man who never was conquered in this game of Shingaukekaūne. That man, during his season of fasting, had a vision, in which he thought that [he?] took it into his head to play the game alone upon the snow crust in a prairie. He got his Shingaukekaūne and threw it upon the snow, when to his great astonishment it turned into a black snake & ran rapidly across to the other side of the prairie. He followed it and found it fast in a large log. He pulled it out, then having assumed its former appearance of a bow, & at the same time a voice came from a large tree near him, saying that he would never be conquered in playing the game.

Shopekenaūminkee — Is a game played with a hundred pieces of small reed or cane about a foot in length. The players seat themselves and one of them takes the hundred sticks between his two hands and lets them drop end wise upon the bark or board where they play. The object of the game is to drop them in such manner as that five pieces, corresponding to the head & limbs, shall fall together. Nothing is counted unless this happens. When one throws out two he remarks, "I have hit him on the legs," and if four, "I have hit his body," and if five, "I have hit him all over" — The throwing out five pieces decides the game & the winner takes possession of the articles staked.

FOOD, MODE OF LIVING &C

There is no animal which they do not use as food; among the fowl, the Raven & Crow only are excepted, to which may be added among aquatic birds, the Loon.

Every kind of fish caught in the neighbouring lakes & rivers is eaten by them as also is the turtle, which is esteemed a delicacy. —

Among the vegetables used by them are —

Paneekēe. The Wild potatoe. These are found in abundance in the wet prairies throughout the country and are gathered in "hoeing time" (June). They are easily boiled and when they wish to change the colour the Indians throw into the kettle a few leaves of the soft maple, which turns them black.

Mukoapīneek. This is the root of the pond lily. It is very tough and requires considerable preparation before it is fit for use. They find it as large as a mans wrist and one to two feet long. After taking up a considerable quantity of it, they dig a hole in the ground, upon the bottom of which they place a layer of stones, On these a layer of wood & on the top another layer of stones. They set the wood on fire, and when it is consumed they cover the heated stones with dry moss, and then throw into the hole the Mukoapīneek. This is covered with grass or moss, and bark, and having filled the hole with water they cover it with earth. They suffer it to remain untouched for five days, when they take out the roots and cut them into small pieces, after which they are dried upon a scaffold & put away for use. They are preserved in this way for a year, and whenever they have use for them, they throw a quantity into the soup kettle before the meat is thoroughly cooked.

Poakshikwileeārkee (the Hollow root), is another root, similar in size to the last mentioned, and found in the same place. It is boiled with meat or eaten raw, and is said to be very palatable.

Keeshikeehaūkee — is the root of a small plant growing in the dry prairies, about six inches in height. The roots are half the size of a mans finger & grow in a cluster. They are boiled & generally eaten with sugar.

Waukeepaaneekēe, grows in bottom lands. It resembles in root & shape of stem, the onion. It is boiled about twelve hours before it is eatable. They are not very fond of it because it produces costiveness.

Waupeesēepina. The white potatoe, is found in low prairies and in appearance & taste is said to resemble our potatoe. It is easily cooked & is considered very good.

These roots are much used by them, particularly in seasons of scarcity.

They have no regular meals, but frequently eat at intervals from morning until night, particularly after hunting or travelling. They seldom eat in the night after laying down to sleep. Each member in the family has a dish & spoon, except the husband & wife, who always eat together and out of the same dish, with the same spoon, using it alternately. Generally the whole family commence at the same time to eat. but no one is obliged to wait until the others choose to pronounce the victuals cooked & their appetites ready, for the kettle is at hand. They generally boil their food, being less troublesome than any other mode of preparing it. —

HUNTING

Their laws of the chase are very liberal. When a man is hunting and kills a deer or other game, or finds a tree containing raccoons, if any one happen along while he is skinning the deer or preparing his game to carry home, he immediately offers to divide it with him, who will accept his offer unless he has already a load. And it often happens that when one has shot a deer he will see at the same moment some other hunter coming towards him, and will immediately abandon his prize, pointing to it as to the property of the person approaching, and will march off to seek some other game.

When two persons are hunting together the one who first wounds an animal is entitled to the skin, but the flesh is equally divided. However it is very common for one to kill an animal & to call the other to skin it, in which case the skin goes to the latter as a compensation for his services. They often form hunting parties, but for no other reason than mutual interest. In these cases the game is all deposited at one place until they go home, when both flesh & skins are equally divided.

There are no ceremonies preceding the departure of a hunting party, or connected with their employment as hunters. —

FEASTS & FASTS

There is no fixed law on the subject of feasting. Almost every family prepares a feast three or four times a year, and during a season of war they sometimes continue them from day to day or from week to week for a considerable time. The feast is considered as an offering to the great Spirit, whom they supplicate for such favours as they need most at the time.

There are no feasts connected with hunting, or upon the planting or ripening of the corn and vegetables, as is practised among the Delawares, nor does the nation tribe or village ever feast together for any purpose whatever. ——

Sickness is sometimes attributed to the neglect of the patients during the season of health, to attend to offering the customary feasts or sacrifices. And when the doctor suggests this cause & finds it true by the confession of the sick man, he directs him to procure a deer, raccoon, or such other animal as he was accustomed to offer, and to atone for his neglect by making a feast. The patient employs some one to hunt the animal for him, another to cook it at night & all night, and another to remain by the kettle and sing. In the morning four or five old men are sent for to partake of the feast and if they cannot eat the whole they take the remains along with them upon their return. The patient generally recovers, when the feast is promptly made. ——

Dog's flesh is seldom used by them in feasts, and is not considered essential on any occasion, but some individuals are in the habit of using it on account of the convenience of procuring the animal.

With one or two exceptions, fasts are only in use among the young — The boys are compelled to black themselves at an early age, say four or five years old, & some younger, and to fast, at first for half a day at a time and afterwards for one two or more days, as the constitution can bear the deprivation of food. When they begin to grow up they continue to fast from a sense of duty, until they are pitied by some animal, who come to them in their dreams and brings relief. They paint themselves black and fast at intervals until they think themselves old enough to assume the rights of a man, when the black paint is exchanged for vermillion &

other ornamental colours and they are considered marriageable. This change of the paints is considered an important era in the life of an Indian. Females fast as well as the men, and for the same reason, but they substitute earth for the coal or black paint which is seen upon their faces at this season. It is said that they adhere more rigidly to the fast than the men.

Neither men or women fast after having sat out in the journey of life, unless it be upon the loss of some very near and dear relative, when they sometimes abstain from food for long intervals during the whole mourning season. —

MISCELLANEOUS

There are among the Miamies, men, who assume the dress and character of women, and abandoning the society of their own sex, associate altogether with the females, taking an equal share in planting, hoeing & gathering the corn, in all the domestic drudgery, and in all other respects adhering strictly to their peculiar manners and employment.

They commence at an early period of life, during the fasting season, and it is said that the adoption of the manners of the other sex is the consequence of having seen in a dream a female, who directed them to do so. They are generally respected in the nation, by both sexes, and the fact of their sex is not kept secret. Sometimes they take advantage of the liberty which is afforded them in their intercourse with the females and carnal connection is not rare.

Instances have been known of these persons going to war; on which occasion the habiliments of the women were exchanged after leaving the village for the warriors dress, and a re-exchange made upon returning to it. These persons are called "Waupeēngwoatar, or The White Face." They are never numerous.

Among those tribes residing upon the Illinois and supposed to have been meant by the french travellers under the general appellation "des Illinois," were the *Piankeshaws*, *Makoateeaūkee* or *Kaskaskias*, both springing from the

Miamies; the *Kickapoos*, of whom one tribe was called *Maskōáteeau*, (or *M'skōáteeau*, "People of the prairie" from *M'skōátaa*, a prairie,) the *Peorias*, who sprung from the *Kaskaskias*, the *Wüyautōnoakee* or *Weēaus*, all more or less connected with the Miamies by marriages; the *Kaūhpaus Aukaūsaus*, *M'whüwauteés*, a branch of the *Osages*, and the *Waushawnoas*. — It is thought that they took their names from some peculiarity in the place of their location.

The Miamies say that the Kickapoos were driven from the east by the Iroquois and Wyandots during a long war, that they passed the Miamies & descended the Wabash to the Wüyautōnoakee with whom they were soon incorporated by intermarriages, that they afterwards intermarried with the Miamies of whom the Wüyautōnoakee were descendants, & that they are now of a mixed breed, of Miami, Weēau & Kickapoos. They further have a tradition, borrowed from the Kickapoos, that long ago a Shawnee boy becoming angry with his brother, who had assumed to himself too great a share of a Bears foot which was cooked for them by their mother, ran away, or separated himself from the tribe, and growing up, formed the present Kickapoo nation, whose language is even at this day understood by the Shawnees.

The Makoateeaūkee Maskōateeau, each means "People of the prairie, the first in Miami & the latter in Kickapoo —

The Kickapoos reside three or four days journey from Terre Haute, between the Wabash & Illinois rivers & are about 400 in number, men, women & children.

The Miamies do not whistle for their children instead of calling them by name.

They know nothing of a nation called Onytanons.[5]

In Miami Makōatawaa and in Kickapoo Maskōataa, means "a prairie."

They have no tradition respecting the deluge.

The word *Mascotens* has been supposed to have some relation to *fire*, but I do not think the suggestion was well

[5] "Onytanons" was one of the French spellings of the name of the tribe called "Weas" by the English and "Weēaus" by Trowbridge.

founded — Makōatawaa & Maskōataa, above mentioned, resemble in their respective dialects, the words *Kōatawaa* & *Skōataa* fire, and from that circumstance I am induced to suppose that the name of prairie originated in a belief of the Indians that they were occasioned by being overrun or burned by fire, or from the custom which they entertained & still entertain of setting fire to them at certain seasons of the year; and that the apparent coincidence above mentioned was thus ascertained.

A TALE — FOUNDED ON FACT
Kiléapwaūkee — Totshemūnamaoo K.[6] *story*

The Kickapoos were never numerous. It is supposed that they are as much so now as they ever were. When they first came to the Wabash, being driven from the east by the hostile nations of that country, two of their young men resolved to set out and travel, to see the surrounding nations and in quest of adventures. They visited the nations east of the Mississippi and then shaped their course westward, continuing their travels upon one of the rivers to a place where the red pipe stone is found (St. Peters). Here they remained a short time, when they prepared again & sat out, continuing the same route. After travelling some time they came to a range of very high mountains in crossing which they travelled nearly half a moon. On the opposite side they met a man bearing in his hand a Pukemaūgun (war club) painted red. He said to them, "I have come to see you," and immediately turned about & retraced his steps. They were not at all intimidated, but continued on. They soon saw another man approach. His pukemaūgun was painted red on one side & black on the other. He made the same speech to them which they had before heard, and left them. He was succeeded by a third with a black pukemaūgun, a fourth with a white one & a fifth with a green one, the latter of whom said, "You will soon arrive" — Presently they came into a prairie at one side of which was a large village. They made towards it, &

[6] Kickapoo.

upon approaching saw two rows of men, extending from the entrance of the village to a large lodge at one extremity. One of the men beckoned to them to advance between the rows and they complied. They entered the lodge and saw it occupied only by one old man. On looking around they perceived $Upeem\overline{ii}$, (beds) extending about the lodge, and at short distances from each other a parcel of Kaupēēnawee (medecine bags) suspended from the sides of the lodge. "Be seated" said the old man; "you see me here alone, my sons have gone to war, and in four nights will return." The young men seated themselves and soon felt at home. Five days after their arrival the scalp yell was heard near the village and the sons of the old man, ten in number, returned with four scalps which they had taken. They were introduced to the two travellers as to their adopted brothers, and very soon became familiar and affectionate towards them. When they had rested from the fatigue of their excursion the old man told them to prepare to go to war again and that their new brothers would assist them. They accordingly prepared and sat out, twelve in number, for the Ohio. Each man had with him one of the Kaupēēnauwee, and a dress to correspond, and when they had left their village they were changed into birds and flew towards the Ohio. They met their enemy there in the form of a four headed hydra or some other animal having four heads, and they vanquished him. Having done this they cut his body in pieces & flew back to the village of the old man, changing their form when they approached. When the two travellers had remained some time the old man presented to each of them a Kaupēēnauwee and gave them permission to depart for their own village, telling them that he was (Tshingweyaū) the Thunder, that they would never see him again, but that they might rely upon his assistance in all their warlike undertakings. After much travelling these young men reached their home, and soon resolved to put to the test the promise of the old man. They went to war, & each of them bro.^t home the number of scalps which he sat out for. Ever since this the Kickapoos have been very brave and very fortunate in war and have paid great veneration to the Kaupeēnawee. They are respected by other tribes and never fail to be well treated wherever they go. —

MONAATOOWAUKĒE—YOUNG TSHINGWÜZAUKEE — THE THUNDER SPIRITS

Very many ages ago one of the Tshingwüzaū or Young Thunder or sons of the Thunder went to the falls of Niagara for the purpose of destroying the Mōnetoo that reigns in that tremendous work of nature, but after a long and very severe conflict he was overpowered, made prisoner, and remains there to this day. A long time after his capture his brothers, ten in number, sat out to rescue him. A Miami was out in the woods and had just levelled his arrow at a fine deer, when a rumbling noize behind him caused the removal of his eye for a moment from the game, & upon looking up he saw coming towards him ten, very large, winged animals apparently half birds, half men. Each of them was armed with an immense Pukemaūgun or War Club, proportioned to the size of the bearer. Nine of these beings passed the Indian without regarding him, but the last one stopped and having interrogated him about his pursuit, success, &c, he drew from his right wing a feather and presented it to the hunter, who upon accepting it immediately became transformed into the shape of his companion. The thunder then disclosed the plan of the party and the object of their excursion, and the hunter having acceded to a proposition to accompany them the two sat out and soon overtook those who had gone before. The hunter and his story, were made known to the warriors by their brother and the whole party proceeded on. When they arrived at the falls, they were much perplexed for a plan by which they might call the attention of the Mōnetoo to such place as would afford them good battle ground. At length he came out himself — a wonderful serpent, of immense size, of black colour and having on his head two horns as large as those of the Elk. The brothers were at first sight intimidated at the frightful appearance of the Mōnetoo, but at length one of them resolved to attack him. He did so, but his Pukemaūgun had no effect. Another succeeded him, but tho' stronger than his brother, the Mōnetoo did not appear to know that any thing was near him but his native rocks & cascade, so little did he regard the oft repeated blows of the warrior. Finally the brothers requested the Miami ally to try the effect of his Pukemaūgun. He approached cautiously, and by a well directed blow he gave the Mōnetoo a death wound. The pain induced by this caused him to writhe & to sigh, and the air was so convulsed by this effort as to occasion an increased noise in the waters around. The Miami was carried by it a great distance off and he fell to the ground with a force which caused a suspension of life. Here his adopted brothers found him. They exerted themselves a little and he recovered sufficiently to accompany them to the battle ground in front of the Mōnetoo's cave where they saw the fallen enemy lifeless. They drew him out of the cave and having separated his head & horns from the body they placed it upon a pole in the same manner that they now serve scalps, and proceeded to return home having first searched in vain for the prisoner their brother. When they reached the place where they had met the Miami they thanked him for his assistance and told him that he was at liberty to return to his friends and enjoy the reputation of the greatest warrior in the nation, or to accompany them as he then was; he chose the former, and surrendering the feather to the person from whom he had received it, he found himself again a human being pursuing the pleasures of the chase. He returned to his village, the people of which had despaired of seeing him again, and having recounted to them the history of the excursion which he had taken, he sat down with the character of the most extraordinary man of his age, and was ever after esteemed a great warrior, with whom it was folly to compete. ———

WŪYAUTŌNOA TOTSHEMŪNAMAOO
A WĒEAU TALE

Many years ago a Wēeau going out to hunt, discovered upon the bank of a small stream a number of human beings, as he supposed, in a crowd, dancing. He approached, and found that they were not men but the *Tshingwüzaūkee manaatoowaūkee* — or Young thunder spirits. They were armed with Pukemaūkunau or War clubs, and told the hunter that they were preparing to attack an enormous Monāatoo, which infested the country and desired his assistance. Accordingly they sat out & soon met with the object of their search, in the form of an immense animal, having large horns like an Elk. They attacked him with their Pukemaūkunau, but the enemey defended himself so adroitly that they could not effect their object, and were just about to abandon the pursuit when two little boys came up and having laughed at them for their weakness, proposed to teach them how to destroy the animal. Accordingly they jumped upon the back of the animal, with great alacrity, and siezed him by his horns. Being alarmed the animal endeavoured to throw off his riders by tossing his head in a most furious manner. But he found this plan ineffectual and at length bethought himself of the expedient of running through a large mountain. So he entered at the foot of the mountain and made his way thro' the earth. But upon coming out at the other side he found himself still incumbered as before. This was but amusement to the boys, and having satisfied themselves with teasing the animal they resolved to finish the business of despatching him. They made some fire and each one took it upon himself to set on fire one of his horns. These soon began to burn, and in a short time the fire proceeded down to the brain and the animal expired, to the great joy of Tshingwüzaūkee, who then returned to their homes.

The Indians were formerly much plagued by the malicious designs of one of these great manitoos, whom they called *Maangeēkunyar, Monāatwau* or Big Boned Monetoo. He dwelt in a difficult & very dangerous pass, in a Buffalo lick, on the war path from the Miami to the Cherokee country, and as he favoured the Cherokees, every other nation that attempted to attack them suffered most severely in the loss of its warriors. Stories are told of 19 out of twenty & thirty out of 40, miami warriors, being killed in attempting to force the pass; And it is said that of upwards of 100 Chippeways who made an excursion into that country, almost every one met death at the big lick.

Among their war stories, they relate the following. A party, consisting of four or five hundred Miami warriors went out to war from their settlement on White River, against some of their southern neighbours, leaving their village in the care of the old decrepid men, their wives and children. Soon after their departure a band of Senecas came suddenly upon the village, and finding it in a defenceless state made prisoners of every remaining inhabitant. They immediately sat out for their own country, leaving none behind but a very old woman, whom they supposed they had killed, but she recovered sufficiently to inform her friends upon their return of the dreadful misfortune which had befallen the nation. The Senecas made a practice of killing and eating one of the Miami children at every nights encampment, and on the following morning they took another very young one and having thrust a stick thro' its head, sat it up in the path with the face towards the Miami town which they had left. They continued to do this every day and when they had arrived within one days march of their village they sent an express to inform their friends of their good fortune and to bid them prepare a great kettle and spoon, for the purpose of enjoying the good broth which they were to bring them. This was accordingly done, and the people of the village were so overjoyed that they could not await the arrival of their warriors, but immediately enkindled a large fire and began to dance around it, enjoying in anticipation the fruits of the excursion. In the mean time the Miami warriors returned to their village, where they heard from the lips of the old woman her tale of woe. They did not hesitate a moment, but sat out in pursuit of the cowardly Senecas, and by dint of great exertion reached their camp on the evening before they expected to enter their village. Each mangled innocent whose body had been placed in the path was recognized by its parent, whose agonized heart almost broke at the sight; but they resolved not to suffer themselves to be prevented by their grief from devising means to obtain an ample revenge. Many of the Senecas were at this time in possession of fire arms, which they had received from the french and in this respect had great advantage over the Miamies. To obviate this difficulty the latter chose not to attack them openly, but resolved to pass them and await in ambuscade their arrival. They accordingly arranged themselves in two rows along the road which the Senecas were to travel and having got fixed they despatched two spies to watch the motions of the enemy. When the spies approached the camp one of the cooks had just cut off the head of a child and was preparing his body for the kettle. Hearing a noise outside of the camp, he tho! that a wolf was probably near, and throwing the head that way, cried out, "there goes the head of a Miami, take it for your supper." The spy approached cautiously and secured the head, which he took back to his companions, who recognized it. Before day the Senecas prepared their burdens & sat out for their village. Each man was heavily loaded with the plunder taken from the Miami camp, and having this on his shoulders over his gun, was illy prepared for immediate defence. They marched in Indian file, as usual, and soon approached the ambuscade of the Miamies. When they had passed so far as to enable them to surround the party the Miami who was in the rear made the cry of an Elk, and at that signal all arose and commenced a furious attack. The Senecas were so much surprised as to be easily overpowered. Every man was killed excepting six, four of whom were taken prisoners and two escaped to carry the news to their village. Of these four two were killed and the Miamies having cut off their heads perforated the ears & putting a bark string through them, put them around the necks of the survivors, whose hands, noses & lips they cut off, telling them to run home and show their friends the vengeance of the Miamies.

As they afterwards learned, the two persons who escaped, fled immediately to the village, crying out, we are undone, lost, killed, throw away your kettle and stop the dance. But no notice was taken of them and the dance continued until the two prisoners so shockingly mangled & bearing the heads of their companions, suspended from their necks, entered the ring. Then all was horror & confusion. The kettle was thrown in one direction and the spoon in another and the dance was changed into raving and horrific extravagancies, at the loss of their fathers, husbands & brothers, whom so lately they heard of in the arms of victory.

The Miamies returned to their village with those of the party whose lives had been spared by the Senecas for the purpose of glutting their inhuman appetites upon their return home.

LE GROS'S ACCOUNT OF THE MEDECINE SOCIETY

Anciently, an old man on the St. Josephs (a Miami) had the misfortune to lose his only son, by a sickness. He was a great favorite, as well with his father as the nation generally. The old man was so grieved at his loss that he was entirely inconsolable, and he determined to leave the place where every object which he saw, reminded him of his misfortune. Accordingly he painted himself black, in token of his intention to fast, and he sat out to travel about the woods, without any other object but to dissipate his grief. He continued to roam and to fast until he had slept 8 nights absent from his village; the ninth night bro! him to the head of the Elk heart river, and he prepared to encamp. He had reclined himself against a tree to sleep, when he heard at a short distance from him the sound of a drum. He arose and went to the place whence the noise proceeded. There he found an immense lodge, extending from east to west, having a door in each end. He hezitated a short time, but at last concluded to enter. He removed the skin from the door and beheld a great concourse of people, in the midst of whom sat the person who beat the drum. An aged and respectable looking man bid him to come in, and pointing to a seat, told him to be seated. He obeyed, and when he had sat down, the other addressed him thus

"Do not think that this visit to us is accidental. You have come here because we wished it. We saw your grief and were desirous to remove it. Your tears have been already partly dissipated, and if you follow the advice which we give you, and do as you see us do, they will be entirely dried and you will grieve no more. The Great Spirit, who put us upon this earth has permitted us to live *half a day*. If you conduct yourself gratefully and pay proper respect to the information we are about to give you, the same privilege will be granted to you. But if you trifle with the secrets which we are going to reveal, rest assured that you will not live until the noon."

Having said this, the ceremonies of initiation commenced. Two men who were sitting at the eastern end of the lodge, arose & walked around, half dancing, half walking, to the right; when they reached the place from which they started, one of them placed himself at the eastern door and stopped. The other continued around to the western door, where he also stopped, standing directly opposite his companion. Then the old [man] who had first spoken got up & going to the western door, he turned around to face the audience, took from this scabbard a kind of knife and throwing back his head, thrust it into his throat up to the hilt. He then walked or ran around the lodge four times, and having done this fell down dead, in the middle. When he had laid there a short time, two others got up and danced around the lodge to the place where the old man laid. They lifted up his body and continued the dance, holding him up by the arms & dragging him along. The fourth time that they had danced around the lodge the old man revived, and his attendants having previously drawn the knife from his throat, he showed no signs of a wound. He then addressed the adventurer, and said — "You tho! probably that I was dead, and so I should have been, had I not taken the precaution to rub some of this medecine upon my knife." He then exhibited some medecine & told the old man that whenever he wished to perform this part of the ceremony he had only to use it and he would be safe from any effect of the knife. This performance being ended, the man at the east end of the lodge danced around four times and then, sticking a knife in his side, he fell down dead. When he had expired, two other men rose, and, taking up his body, carried it around the lodge four times, when he revived, as the other had done, And addressing the visitor explained to him the kind of root which had saved him from the effect of the knife.

This one was succeeded by two old women, who rose from the east end of the lodge and danced around once, to the music of their own song. Then one of them transformed herself into a bear, and continued to go around the lodge, dancing, to the great amusement of all who saw her clumsy gait, four times. She then reassumed her natural shape and addressing the noviciate, showed him the root which had enabled her to perform this wonder. She further taught him the use of the root by which a person who has any malice against another, may send, no matter how great the distance, a little agent to torment him that this root by being chewed, became a ball of fire, and while the person who caused its existence, was smoking his pipe, it would go and perform the task imposed upon it. When her task was thus fulfilled she sat down, and was succeeded by her companion, who transformed herself into a panther, and after dancing around the lodge four times, as the other had done, stopped before the old man and communicated to him the knowledge of the root which enabled her to effect this transformation, giving him at the same time power to use it. She further showed him and gave him a root, by use of which he could change himself into a large owl and fly swiftly to the habitation of any one who should injure him; where he would appear like a ball of fire to the guilty person, and effect his punishment as should please him. She gave him a pipe, and told him that when he wished to go any where, he must fill that, and he would accomplish his journey and return, before the pipe would be emptied, so rapidly would he travel.—

Then these two women desired another, from the west

end of the lodge, to perform something on her part, for the instruction of the stranger. Accordingly she arose, and having danced four times around the lodge she was suddenly transformed into an ugly looking animal, which seemed to be much inflated with wind. This animal vomited up a small black substance, and then turned itself to the old man and said "You probably want to know what I am. These people whom you see call me momaukeēseeau, or the Toad. With the smallest particle of this black substance I can destroy all my enemies. I give you now the same power of transformation and use of this poison, which I possess, and I demand as an equivalent, that when you return to your own village you shall immediately put your skill in practice, by giving a small portion of the poison to one of the most lovely and esteemed young men there, that I may have a piece of him to eat. And when you are injured by any person, if he be very distant from you, it will only be necessary to draw his figure upon the earth, and make in the proper place the form of his heart. Then you must procure a swallow feather and having dipped it in some of this black medecine, apply it to the heart, and your enemy will immediately die. Or if you desire that he should linger in pain & torment some time, you may effect that by putting the poison on one of the limbs, remote from the vitals. This poison, is not of roots, but simply my breath."

Another woman, from the west end of the lodge, followed this one, who still retained the shape of Toad. This latter, after dancing twice around the lodge, fainted away. Two others immediately repaired to her assistance, lifted her up, carried or dragged her twice around the lodge and she revived, at the same time vomiting forth a small white shell (the *pucelle* of the french & *pawpaw* of the negroes) called *Tshaūkoaseesee*. Then she walked or danced around twice, holding the shell in the palm of her hand, and exhibiting it to the members.

The toad again addressed our old man, drew his attention to the event before his eyes and invested him with the power to use the *Tshaūkoaseesee* in all its forms. She told him that having this in his breast, he would have long life and good health & that he could transform himself into a mink, snake, mouse or bird, for the purpose of entering houses and seeing & hearing what was there going forward. And that he would use it also in the ceremony of shooting each other in the lodge.

The Members of the lodge then made a signal for one of their body, called M'saalārtsha, to come. *M'saalārtsha* is one of the principal Meetāawaa, and resides on the opposite side of the sea. He heard the signal & came, and when he approached the lodge each step that he took caused the earth to shake under him. When he had entered & danced twice around the lodge, he swallowed a barbed arrow, for the satisfaction of those present, and almost immediately dropped down & died, the blood gushing from his mouth in large streams. But the exertions of three or four who took him up & danced around the lodge with him, bro't him to life, and he then made our old man acquainted with the roots which he used to prevent death from following the extraordinary exertion of swallowing an arrow.

Then he danced around the lodge again and threw himself into a large blasing fire, which was enkindled in the lodge, and after having rolled about some time he got up in a blaze and ran or danced around the circle. He then shewed the old man the roots which would preserve him from being burned, in case he should ever wish to astonish the spectators of his feats.

This ended *M'saalārtshar's* part of the performance, and he then called upon the members generally, to exhibit, each his particular power, for the benefit of the old man. Whereupon one from the south side of the lodge jumped up, and having danced around twice, as was customary with all, he laid himself down in the middle of the lodge, upon his back. Two men then went to him & with a knife, cut open his body, from the chin downward. Thus exposed they showed him to the old man and then by chewing a root which they exhibited, & rubbing it over the body & the wound (like Don Quixote sticking plaster) they revived the subject, whose body shewed no marks of incision whatever. This man then transformed himself into a Beaver, and addressing our stranger, gave him the knowledge of this important root, and the power to transform himself into a Beaver, and seek out his enemies, at the same time having the power to conceal himself under the water. Another man then rose, and having danced around twice, he stopped at the middle of the lodge & gave a kick at the earth — Immediately he turned into a Turkey buzzard, and said to the old man, that whenever he wished to pursue his enemies he might take this form, and if when he arrived at the house of a man whom he wished to punish, he did not see his victim, he had only to fly twice around the house & he would appear.

This man was succeeded by one who placed himself at the western door of the lodge & addressed the old man thus. "My friend, attend to me. You see I am changing into a Lizzard. Listen & I will teach you how to profit by my example. Whenever you wish to go in this form to kill any enemy, you must eat some of this root which I show you, and your transformation will be immediate. You will never have difficulty in approaching your enemy, but have a care, that as soon as you have killed him you will possess yourself of his tongue, a thumb and little toe. Here is a small stone & here a piece of root. When you wish to make fire rub these together, and when the fire is enkindled, take the tongue, thumb & toe & cook & eat them. They are delicious eating. Besides if eaten for my sake I shall enjoy them much. This must be done before you leave his lodge."

Another arose at the north side of the lodge and commended his bretheren for their promptness in instructing their friend, whom they had called there out of pity for his griefs and for the purpose of teaching him how they lived. He then changed himself successively into a fox, wild cat, and mole & rabbit, and taught the novitiate the use of the several roots by which he accomplished this, adding that he might choose any one of these forms, when he designed to visit an enemy & compass his destruction, but that he must always watch the grave of the object of his wrath and steal thence a piece of the tongue to make a feast of, in praise of the animal whose appearance he had adopted. The novitiate now began to discover that what he had supposed to be men, in the lodge, were beasts & birds of every description, which to his vision had the appearance of human beings. The old man, for such we must still call him, who bore the principal part in the ceremony of instruction, then addressed the novitiate. "Now, said he, you see the reason of our calling you here. We saw you very much afflicted, and were disposed to relieve your troubles. The power which has been given you, and the ceremonies which you have seen, are half bad and half good: that is to say, men will be disposed to divert them to purposes equally vicious & laudable. When you go home you will find this to be a valuable profession, and we enjoin it upon you to keep it secret from the world. You will have the authority to form a new branch of this society, but you must never initiate members, without a heavy fee; and have a care that you do not bring the society into disrepute, by extending it too much. Conduct every part of the ceremony with gravity and secrecy and suffer no one to contemn it or to ridicule its proceedings. And now as you have seen all the first part of our ceremonies, and have possessed yourself of our powers, we intend to show you more." The visitor looked around him and beheld upon the walls of the lodge a great number of the skins of beasts & birds, which he was told were the Kaupēēnauwee, or Medecine bags. The *Mitaawaukee* then prepared eight small sweat houses in the centre of the grand lodge, and arranged them in a row — "These, said he, are *Noazeekonēē* or *Sweat houses*, and here you must retire when you wish to obtain a great favor from the great Spirit, or to perform any of the wonderful actions for which we have empowered you. The first description of the Noazeekonēē is common & small, as you see, but the last one, which you see suspended or floating in the air, without any support, is that kind in which you are to perform the most important professional actions. — You have been with us now four days,* and it is time for you to return to your friends.

When he had finished, the novitiate prepared himself to go, and turning to bid farewell to his friendly instructors he saw nothing but bears, panthers, Beavers and the other animals and things which had been succesively represented to him. He approached the door of the lodge and withdrew, when, to his great surprise he found himself just rising from the bottom of a lake. He made his way to the shore and commenced his journey homeward. When he reached his village, which had undergone but little alteration in his absence, the night had come on & he entered his own lodge unobserved. The noise of his entrance awaked his wife, who demanded the cause of such an untimely visit. He made himself known and embraced his family. On the following morning his first care was to make a small sweat house near his lodge. — There he secluded himself, and when the news that the lost man was found, reechoed throughout the village, one of his uncles came to congratulate him. He admitted him to his sweat house, & after receiving his promise of secrecy, acquainted him with the history of his absence.

Arrangements were made for the initiation of his uncle, and on the following day they retired to a remote & secret corner of the wood, and prepared a small lodge for the ceremony. Here the Mitāāwau stretched himself upon a skin, and transformed himself into each of the different animals & birds used in the grand lodge, at the same time instructing his uncle in all the mysteries pertaining thereto.

When he had finished he told his uncle that by a proper use of the secrets of their art, they would not only please their patrons, from whom the power was derived, but would ensure to themselves long life and the enjoyment of the

* I have often observed that in relating their stories, or in important speeches, they use this as a figurative expression, meaning by the term *day*, a year. So it is intended in this case.

good things of the world — And that if any person applied for admission, he must undergo instruction for four years, preparatory to his initiation, during which time he must make occasional presents to them, by way of a douceur.

It was not long before their neighbours began to know that these two persons possessed the knowledge of some secret art, and a man & woman applied for admission. They were immediately taken to a remote place in the wood and put under a course of instruction and in due time made members, having received the powers of the members by regular degrees or gradations, as, for instance, at the first lesson, the power to swallow a knife, at the second that of imitating the noise of a wolf, at the third, the capacity to assume the form of that animal. Then these four tho.t proper to exhibit before the people. They accordingly formed a long lodge, and on the following day their noise & dancing attracted the notice of the villagers, who were much pleased with their performances & many of whom became members.

Wisekaukaūtshe, or Cold feet,[7] who lived many ages ago, was one of the most distinguished & powerful members of this society — He frequently amused himself with the different changes which he was able to produce by dint of his professional power. Sometimes he passed the village in the form of a Bear, a Buffalo or a Buck, and when the young hunters had chased him a mile or two, they would find him in his natural shape, sitting by a spring, or on the bank of the river. At length the other Members of the Society became so jealous of him that they resolved upon his death — They often invited him to meetings of the Society, where by their united powers they would destroy him and burn his body; but they always found him soon afterwards, at his house, engaged in a conversation as if nothing had happened. At length they found from his son, who was also a member that the old man had a secret medecine bag, sowed in his clothes.

[7] There was a Miami chief named Coldfoot or Le Pied Froid mentioned in many of the French documents about the middle of the eighteenth century, but he died of smallpox.

They possessed themselves of this, and then proposed to the old fellow a trial of their strength at lifting a great rock. When he had taken it up, they caused him to fall, & the weight of his burden crushed him to death. Then they burned his body, and on the following morning nothing was seen in the ashes, but an immense number of toads, lizards and such small reptiles. The Son, who was much incensed at the treatment of his father, prepared a grand medecine, by which he destroyed all the conspirators. As they were the principals of their respective bands, and the remaining members were not fully empowered, the Society has not been so formidable since that event, and they have entirely lost the power of transformation.

The name *Mitaawau* is said to have been received from the original founders of the society, and is not used, but in application to it. All the roots & stuff used or pretended to be used by them is called *Medecine* or *Maungeeshee*. They don't pretend to account for the manner in which other nations have received these mysteries. Each root used in the Society has a particular song, and, to use their own language, a song is as distinctly designated by the root to which it belongs as the songs of the whites by their paper & black marks. They have no musick boards or hieroglyphicks in this society. —

The society is divided into small lodges or branches, containing from four to 10 members. Application for admission may be made to any member of one of the lodges, who informs his fellows, and at a given time the applicant brings his initiatory fee, and in a sweat house remote from the village, receives his instructions. He is afterwards publickly acknowledged as a member, at one of the meetings of the society. These are held four or five times during the year, sometimes for the purpose of receiving members, at others only to practice their arts. They are often numerously attended as well by the neighbouring nations as by those of the nation giving the feast but none except members of the society are invited or suffered to partake in the ceremonies.

The Menōaminies acknowledge the reception of the knowledge of the Meetāawau from Moneebōozhoa. This character is familiar to the Miamies & has a correspondent in Misaalārtshar, who is mentioned in the preceding account.

Misaalārtsha formerly resided in the west, where he passed his time in company with the two Little boy manitoos. When, on a certain occasion the Tshingwüzaukee, or young thunder spirits, were going to the East, he prayed to be taken along. He was a very obstreperous manaātwun and they did not like his company, but as he engaged to comport himself well and never to wink when passing over a village, they consented that she [he] should go along. They accordingly gave him one of their feathers and he changed into a bird & flew with them, but he could not keep his promise, for every village he came to he winked, & the lightning, from his eyes so frightened the inhabitants, that when the thunders arrived on the opposite side of the sea, they determined to leave him there. And so they took away from [him] the feather which had been given and came off. He has since visited this island only on very great occasions, such as the one just related.

The Meetāawau profess no power over the whites, because the latter have such hard skins in consequence of their great use of salt.

They do not possess any signs, by which they can communicate with each other.

The Little Turtle is not considered a Miami. A frenchman, who traded from the Mississippi to the Lakes, purchased in the west an Iowau girl and adopted her as his daughter. In one of his subsequent visits from Montreal he employed a Mohiccan Indian, partly civilized to accompany him in capacity of a servant. In the Kickapoo country the master & man became engaged in a battle and the former was wounded in the thigh. The Mohiccan carried him, with incredible labour & fatigue to the Miami village and when he had reached there the grateful frenchman poured out his lamentations because he had lost all his goods and had no means to reward him. The Mohiccan offered to accept of the Iioawau girl & the other consented. They were married, settled among the Miamies & had a great many children, of whom the eldest was Little Turtle.

MANGEUR D'HOMME
AMAUMOAWEEAUKEE
MAN EATERS[8]

From the extreme reluctance to acknowledge any connection, however distant, with this society, I have found it difficult to obtain any thing like a distinct account of it. At length however I have prevailed upon Le Gros to communicate all that he knows respecting its origin and laws.

When the Mi. resided at St. Josephs, ab! one half of them were known under the name of Mashokeeaūkee and the others as Shōngiseeaukee, two great distinctions, which exist at this day.[9] They were then in the habit of making war upon the Cherokees. A party made an excursion & meeting one of the enemy killed him & left him laying on the ground. When they repassed they saw a wolf & a crow engaged in devouring the body. They communicated this information to their friends at home and described the apparent pleasure of these in such strong terms that their friends tho! it would be fortunate if they could have the same appetite. Two men began to fast soon after, to know what would be the will of the great spirit on this subject. After fasting 15 days one of

[8] "There are men and women that might be called man-eaters because they never fail to eat of all those who are put to death in their villages," wrote Deliette, who was among the Illinois from 1687 until 1698 and with the Miamis the next four years, "Memoir concerning the Illinois Country," *Coll. Ill. State Hist. Library*, 23 (1934): 386.

[9] These would appear to be phratries from the description given of them in the section entitled "Government," but in an account of the "man-eating society," written by Cass and published as an appendix to Henry Whiting's poem *Ontwa, the Son of the Forest* (New York: Wiley and Halstead, 1822), pp. 132–36, it is stated that the membership was confined to the Bear family, and that the number of members was usually fifteen to twenty. He also gave the name of the society as "Ons-e-won-sa."

them had a vision. He saw a man coming towards him, the blood running down at the sides of his mouth. He addressed the dreamer and told him that he was the wolf who had been seen eating a cherokee, and that he would empower him to do so likewise, giving him at the same time an assurance of assistance in war.

The other Miami had a similar vision, in which the crow appeared to him and told him a like story, and further promised that whenever the Miamies procured and ate a prisoner, he & the wolf would be present and assist them.

These dreams being related to their friends, of the Shōngi-seeaukee, a party went again to war against the Cherokees: four prisoners were taken & bro! to the village. One of them being tied to a post in the centre of the ring, the first dreamer asked a woman which part she would take; she replied, a piece from the left hip. Another chose the right hip & his companion the left shoulder, so that the right was left to himself. Each having taken a small piece, the whole party began to dance around & burn the prisoner with brands, and when he gave up the ghost, they ordered a woman to put the kettle upon the fire. Then they took down the prisoner & skinned him, after which they cut his body in pieces and boiled it. When cooked, the men arranged themselves on the west side of the kettle & the women on the east and ate up its contents.

Another prisoner was given to the Mashoakeeaukee, who stood at a distance, silent spectators of the scene. They accepted the present, kept him a short time & sent him to his friends. The two others were adopted. All the Shōngi-seeaukee are members of the society which [is] an inheritable office, descending thro' the mother in case of intermarriages. None of the Mashokeeau[-kee] belong to it.

They are pleased to procure prisoners and none have the power to release them after being once surrendered. Many persons of the Miamies are descendents of the members of this society, tho' they will not confess it. Children were taught to eat with their parents. —

They discontinued the practice about 40 years ago, in consequence of a young woman having dreamed during her fast that she saw a M̄onaatewau who showed her a large fire on which were piled the bodies of her ancestors, members of the society, suffering there for their participation in the crime during life.

They removed their victims to a remote place when about to sacrifice them.

Asking Le Gros what idea the Ind. entertained about the many comforts which the whites possessed over them, such as horses, cattle, sheep, Ducks Geese, Potatoes &c — He says "we have our Bear for your hogs, Buffalo, cattle, Deer for sheep; wild roots for potatoes & our geese & Ducks Your Horses came from the east — Ours with long ears, from the west.

TABLE OF PHONETIC VALUES

[i]	ee......	waubenaūhkee
	ēē......	Wēēau
	ü......	Wüyantonoa
[ı]	e......	waubenaūhkee
[e]	i......	mūkisinee
	ī......	mukoapīneek
[a]	a......	kaupēēnawee
	aa......	olaanaūzwaunaukee
	āā......	nāāpeenwēēk
	u......	mukoapīneek
	ū......	mūkisinee
[ä]	ar......	Meearmēē (the *r* is intrusive)
[ā]	ā......	tshetshākoa
	au......	Wēēau
	aū......	kaūpeeau
	ār......	poakshikwilesārkee (the *r* is intrusive)
[o]	o......	shopekanaūmiukee
[ō]	ō......	maamezhōmoalon
	oo......	keehkoolee paakaumwut
	ōō......	Moneebōōzhoa
	oa......	peepoanwēē
	ōa......	aayōangee